Responding to violence

a collection of papers relating to child sexual abuse and violence in intimate relationships

This book contains papers previously published in the *International Journal of Narrative Therapy and Community Work* (formerly known as *Dulwich Centre Journal*).

Dulwich Centre Publications
ADELAIDE, SOUTH AUSTRALIA

ISBN 0 9577929 7 2

Copyright © 2003 by
Dulwich Centre Publications
Hutt St PO Box 7192
Adelaide 5000, South Australia
phone (61-8) 8223 3966, fax (61-8) 8232 4441
email: dcp@senet.com.au
website: www.dulwichcentre.com.au

Typeset & Layout: Jane Hales

Printed and manufactured by
Graphic Print Group, Richmond, South Australia.

Contents

Contents (cont'd)

Part Three: Working with men who perpetrate violence

Introduction

The last twenty years have seen a sea-change in attitudes towards child sexual abuse and violence in intimate relationships. Whereas once within the professional world these topics were rarely considered, the feminist challenge has resulted in widespread responses to those who have been subjected to this violence and the development of new ways to work with those who perpetrate it.

It is thirteen years since we first published a collection of papers on the issue of sexual violence[1] and a book dedicated to work with men who are violent and abusive[2]. Since that time we have regularly published writings by practitioners working in these areas.

This book consists of a diverse collection of thoughtful practice-based papers that we have recently published in the *International Journal of Narrative Therapy and Community Work* (formally *Dulwich Centre Journal*). The papers in the first section of the book focus on ways of working with those who have experienced child sexual abuse, while those in the second section focus on violence in intimate relationships. The third section describes ways of working with men and young men who have enacted violence.

With violence within families and towards children continuing to affect the lives of so many people, we have great respect for those who dedicate their working lives to addressing this issue. We hope the papers in this collection will offer to you a sense of companionship and hopefulness in your work.

Cheryl White,
Dulwich Centre Publications.

Notes

1. Durrant, M & White, C. (eds) 1990: *Ideas for Working with Sexual Abuse.* Adelaide: Dulwich Centre Publications (now out of print).
2. Jenkins, A. 1990: *Invitations to Responsibility: The therapeutic engagement of men who are violent and abusive.* Adelaide: Dulwich Centre Publications.

1.

Narrative ways of working with women whose lives have been affected by child sexual abuse

by

Sue Mann & Shona Russell [1]

Introduction

Our interest in writing this paper is two-fold. Firstly, to honour the histories, stories and hopes of women who have been subjected to child sexual abuse and to bring some of their knowledges to the foreground. Secondly, as therapists who have a keen interest in narrative practices, we wish to relate how various maps of narrative therapy support our work – in particular, the 'Statement of position map', the stages of 'Definitional ceremony' and 'outsider-witness practices'. Woven through the description of the ways these maps shape our practice, a range of commitments will be articulated that are informed by feminism, poststructuralism and ethical positions that examine relations of power.

Before we begin, we would like to acknowledge two understandings upon which this work is based. The first relates to contexts of power. The work which we do acknowledges that child sexual abuse occurs in a broader context of adult power over children and inequitable gender relations. Child sexual abuse can only occur due to an imbalance in relations of power and involves adults breaking a position of trust and responsibility for the care and protection of children (Joy 1999; O'Leary 1998). The second understanding that significantly shapes our work is in relation to matters of identity. Our work is strongly influenced by the view that identity is socially constructed, that is to say that the meanings that people give to their experiences of life constitute and are shaping of their life (Burr 1995; White 1997). The understanding that identity is socially constructed highlights for us, in our conversations with women, the significance of the historical, cultural and social context of life.

This paper does not represent a full account of therapy with women in relation to child sexual abuse.[2] Instead it attempts to convey how, in our conversations with women survivors of child sexual abuse, we are engaging with particular narrative practices.

Part I: Statement of position map

by
Sue Mann

In this first section of the paper, I (SM) briefly describe the 'Statement of position map' and how this map supports my thinking and practice in working with women who have been subjected to child sexual abuse. In doing so I draw upon examples of my work at Adelaide Central Mission in the child sexual abuse team and tell parts of the stories of my work with four women who I have chosen to name here as Antje, Janet, Natalie and Julie.

To begin, I offer here a brief outline of the 'Statement of position map'. Following this I link each element of the map to my work with women in relation to the effects of child sexual abuse.

Stages of the 'Statement of position map'

As Michael White has described elsewhere (White 2002), there are four stages to the 'Statement of position map':

Stage one: *Negotiation of an experience-near, non-structuralist definition of the problem*

This initial stage involves collaboratively negotiating an experience-near externalised definition of the problem. This negotiation of an externalised definition makes many things possible. Perhaps most significantly, it moves the problem out of the realm of 'expert professional knowledges' and back into a realm within which the person's own solution knowledges can be utilised. For instance, a woman who has previously received a diagnosis of 'social phobia' may, through a process of negotiating an experience-near definition of the problem, come to identify the problem as 'the effects of the voices of terror and panic'. While a description of 'social phobia' leaves little room for action – except to seek assistance from someone with professional expertise in dealing with phobias – the particular woman may already have some skills and knowledges which may be relevant in dealing with the effects of terror and panic. Through further conversations these skills and knowledges may be able to be re-engaged with and further developed.[3]

Questions that might inform this stage of the map might include:

- As we've been talking, you've mentioned these words in relation to your experience of this problem … (insert words here). I'm wondering what name you'd give to this problem?

- Does this name for the problem fit for you or are there other words that better describe this problem and the way it works?

In instances where a professional experience-distant definition of the problem is in existence, other sorts of questions might be relevant:

- What do you mean exactly when you say (e.g. social phobia)? Can you describe that a bit more?

- What do you think of when you say … (e.g. social phobia)?

- Can you help me to understand what you mean by … (e.g. social phobia)?

or,

- In my experience, there are many different types of social phobias. Can you tell me a bit more about what you experience of this and perhaps we could come up with a more precise name …

Stage two: *Mapping the effects of the externalised problem*

The second stage of the 'Statement of position map' involves identifying, naming and mapping out the effects or influence of the problem in the person's life. What we hear about and enquire about in this stage of the map is the person's knowledge of the effects of the problem in their life. This enquiry creates a structure in which to frame knowledge about the influence of the problem, its operation, where and when it has been most and least influential, and over what period of time. We may also enquire as to the effects of the problem on people's relationships with others and their relationship with themselves.

In exploring the effects of the problem, we might ask questions like:

- What effect does 'the panic' have on your relationships with others?

- What effect does it have on your view of yourself at home or when you are working (or in other relevant contexts)?

- What effect does 'the panic' have on your relationship with ...?

- Have these effects changed over time?

- Is 'the panic' always as strong?

- Are there times when it is less influential? If so, when?

Stage three: *Evaluating the effects*

In stage three, we enquire about the person's own evaluation of these effects; whether these effects have been good or bad, okay or not okay for them to have in their life. In inviting such an evaluation of the effects of a problem in a person's life, we actively centre the experience and knowledge of the person who is consulting with us. By not offering our own interpretations and evaluations, and by not identifying the problem from our own perspective, we actively place the person consulting us as the primary author of the experiences of their life.

Questions that might feature in this stage invite an evaluation of the effects of the problem:

- Would you say that 'the panic' is useful, or not useful, or something else?

- Has the idea of 'x' been a good or bad thing to have in your life, or something else altogether?

- It may seem obvious but I wanted to check with you if 'the x' has been good or bad, or maybe a bit of both, or something else?

What you may notice in these questions is that space is opened for evaluations that aren't necessarily about either/or choices and leave options for complexities of experience.

Stage four: *Justification of the evaluation*

The final stage of the 'Statement of position map' involves inviting a justification of the evaluation that has just been made. In inviting a justification of the evaluation, that is to say by asking why the person has evaluated the effects in the way that they have, we open up space for the people consulting with us to give voice to the values, beliefs and intentions that inform those justifications. Asking 'why' a person has evaluated the effects of the problem in the ways in which they have often brings forth important stories or experiences that have never been spoken about before.

In summary, the four stages of the 'Statement of position map' are as follows:

Stage one: *Negotiation of an experience-near, non-structuralist definition of the problem*

Stage two: *Mapping the effects of the externalised problem*

Stage three: *Evaluating the effects*

Stage four: *Justification of the evaluation*

I have tried here to briefly describe how this map can be used to engage with the problems that a person may be experiencing. It also seems important to note that the practices of this 'Statement of position map' support my thinking not only in relation to an enquiry about the problem and its effects, but also in relation to preferred identity conclusions. By following the same stages of the map, orientated to unique outcomes rather than problems, this enables the development of richly described alternative stories.

Having briefly outlined the 'Statement of position map', I would now like to relate the use of this map specifically to work with women survivors of child sexual abuse.

Centering women's experience and knowledge

One of the reasons why I choose to engage with the 'Statement of position map' in my work is that it supports my intention as a therapist to centre women's experience and knowledge in the conversations we share. This is particularly important to me in working with the effects of child sexual abuse where the operations of power by an adult in relation to a child have invariably had the effect of: silencing women from speaking about the abuse; disconnecting them from a sense of being able to influence their own lives; and separating them from trusting their own knowledge and judgement. Often these women consult therapists because the effects of abuse are continuing to operate in their lives. For instance, feelings of shame, blame, and anxiety may be continuing to disrupt their lives. One of the women who has been consulting with me specifically asked me to include in this paper what it was like for her to speak to a therapist about the abuse that had occurred in her life. She wanted readers to know that she came to the therapy room with 'terror and courage'. As she described it, to open up and say something was 'an incredibly brave and huge thing to do'.[4]

The 'Statement of position map' strongly supports me in adopting a respectful position to hear and make space for the storying of the effects of abuse in circumstances where there has been a long history of silencing and shame.

I'll now offer some more detailed examples to illustrate the four stages of the 'Statement of position map'.

Stage one: *Negotiating an externalised definition of the problem*

As mentioned above, the intention within the first stage of the map is to develop an accurate description of the meaning of abuse in the woman's life through the negotiation of an externalised definition of the problem. This is important because frequently when women come to speak to me about their experience of abuse as a child, they come with convincing negative beliefs about themselves. For example, women who have consulted me have described themselves as 'an angry bitch', as 'always sad', as 'depressed', as 'unmotivated'. These are terms which these women believe describe them totally. To renegotiate the naming of these problems in ways that aren't totalising of the women concerned opens many possibilities.

One of the joys and encouragements for me in this work has been to witness the effects on women's lives of externalising the problem in a way that fits more with their own understanding and experience.

Antje, who is 23, came to meet with me about her experience of sexual abuse as a young child of ten. She had only recently spoken for the first time about her experience of abuse, to a friend who had encouraged her to go to counselling. Antje described herself to me as depressed and told me that she had always been miserable. What's more, Antje believed that because the abuse she experienced wasn't as bad as the abuse endured by some others, that her depression and sense of misery was probably due to the kind of person she was. She also told me that she was beyond repair, that she couldn't stop crying, and that she had started to have thoughts of self-harm. At this point, Antje's sense of despair and my own sense of urgency about this sense of despair threatened to take over our conversation.

Through following the map, I wondered with Antje about whether she had considered a collective name for all of these powerful thoughts she had about herself. Was there a particular name that would suit her better than another? Initially, she didn't think there was one, but after some quiet consideration, she offered that she might call them 'the misery thoughts'. This naming of 'the misery thoughts' invited Antje into a different experience of herself. She was no longer describing herself as a miserable kind of person but as someone affected by 'misery thoughts'. In naming 'the misery thoughts', Antje also became much more actively involved in reviewing the effects of these thoughts in her life and the history of these effects. What followed was a considerably different discussion that had Antje's own knowledge, experience and wisdom in relation to the ways 'the misery thoughts' operated in her life at the centre of our collaborative efforts.

I have drawn on this example because it reminds me of how convincingly problem stories can speak to women survivors of child sexual abuse, and also how they can speak to us as therapists. When there was a risk of despair taking over the conversation, what assisted was the process of negotiating an externalised definition of the problem. This created some room for Antje to express her own position in relation to the problem and its effects on her life.

Women who have consulted with me in the past have been very clear about what it means for them to begin to talk about and deal with the effects of child sexual abuse. As a result, when women begin to name abuse and its effects on their lives, I want to create space for the voice of women to be heard and listened to. Women have repeatedly reported that to rush this initial process, or for me as the therapist to move ahead of the woman concerned by imposing a naming of the problem, or alternatively for me to step into 'noticing the positives' rather than fully acknowledging the real effects of the abuse, are all acts which replicate experiences for women of not being heard. They are also acts which devalue, reinterpret or ignore the women's own knowledge and judgement about their lives, and this can be experienced as a further abuse of power. From the feedback of women survivors, I have come to learn of the importance of making space and time to hear about the significant effects of abuse in the women's lives and to ensure that in no way am I minimising these effects. Negotiating an externalised experience-near definition of a problem seems an important way of valuing the women's stories and experiences without getting lost in territories of despair.

I want to also briefly describe another example of stage one of the 'Statement of position map', particularly in relation to developing an externalised definition of the problem when a woman comes to counselling with a professional definition of the problem that may involve notions of inner damage and pathology.

'Post-traumatic stress disorder' has been a term that I have recently been hearing more about in the counselling room. For many women who meet with me, it has been a relief to be given this diagnosis by professional people as it has provided them with a socially sanctioned acknowledgement that their experience of abuse as a child was a trauma. For some women this has made it more possible for them to talk about their distress to others, even if the actual abuse remains un-named. For some, the description 'post-traumatic stress disorder' has been a way of clearly naming the significant physical and emotional effects that the abuse has had on their lives. When women describe themselves as suffering from 'post-traumatic stress disorder', I am interested in how this naming fits for the women. In inquiring about this, I am not suggesting that child sexual abuse is not experienced as traumatic by the women. In my conversations with women I often bear witness to the effects of painful memories and the silencing effects of fear and terror. What is important for me is to make space for this trauma to be understood as having occurred in a context of history and culture. If this is overlooked, then a definition of the problem as 'post-traumatic stress disorder' can become totalising of the woman and internalised by her. When this occurs, women can be vulnerable to further self-blame in relation to not being 'resilient' or 'strong' enough. While never underestimating the extent of the trauma experienced by the women, I have frequently found that there are opportunities to renegotiate a naming of the problem in ways that resonate more with women's experiences of life. This was certainly true for Natalie.

Natalie arrived for one of our meetings with news that the Mental Health Services, who had been supporting her for some time, had told her that they thought her symptoms were a sign of 'post-traumatic stress disorder'. In enquiring about what this naming was like for Natalie, it was not my intention to discredit another professional or to privilege my own thinking, but to acknowledge that naming problems in such a way has effects, and to consider whether this was a name that suited Natalie. Natalie told me it was okay to have this new diagnosis from the Mental Health Services because she thought it was better than borderline personality disorder, a diagnosis which they had previously considered giving her. She was however a bit puzzled by what 'post-traumatic stress disorder' meant and thought it had something to do with the nightmares, sleeping problems, fear and anxiety that she had been experiencing. I asked Natalie whether there was another name that might suit her better or whether it was okay to stay with the term 'post-traumatic stress disorder'. Natalie responded with barely a second's hesitation. She said that she'd have called it the 'I've had a lot of shit in my life disorder'. We then made a list of 'the shit' that had happened in her life which included abuse by her uncle, removal from her family to foster care, ill health, self-harm, homelessness, further sexual abuse as an adult, and addiction. This new naming of the problem enabled a conversation that focused on the nightmares as an effect of abuse rather than as a symptom of 'post-traumatic stress disorder', and with this discernment came the beginnings of an increased sense of personal agency. Natalie began to develop ideas about ways of influencing the place that the nightmares had in her life.

Naming problems as external to people, in ways that have personal and direct meaning in their lives, can create a certain linguistic space. This space can then enable women to bring their own agency to a conversation about the effects of child sexual abuse.

Stage two: *Mapping the effects of the externalised problem*

The second stage of the 'Statement of position map' involves exploring the effects of the externalised problem. I am interested in hearing what the women know and understand about the way in which the experience of child sexual abuse has affected their lives. And I also want to check with them that I have understood correctly and clearly what these effects have been, as this checking and clarifying often leads to a further thickening of the meaning of these effects in the lives of the women. It is this exploration of the effects of abuse that often exposes the relations of power in which the abuse occurred. It is also this exploration that enable these effects to be re-named as effects of abuse.

What is more, as women begin to identify the effects of the abuse on their sense of themselves, the thin conclusions that they have about their lives (e.g. 'an angry bitch', 'always sad', 'depressed', 'unmotivated') begin to be understood as the effects of abuse rather than the reality about their own identity.

Mapping the effects of the externalised problem also provides a way of hearing about and acknowledging the special knowledge of the women. We come to hear not only about the women's knowledge of the effects of the abuse but invariably also about some of the strategies and skills that they have for managing these effects. Just as the effects of abuse may have been present in their lives for many years, so too have ideas and know-how about limiting the influence of these effects. This kind of conversation, in which the therapist is consulting the woman about the effects of the externalised problem, keeps the women's knowledge at the centre of our work, and this enables them to articulate the complexity and specifics of their experience.

For example, let me return to Antje. Her naming of the problem as 'the misery thoughts' led to a rich development of her insider knowledge of the tactics of these misery thoughts and of her strategies to manage them.

The kind of questions that supported this enquiry were:

- *What effects do these misery thoughts have on your thinking about yourself?*

- *What has been the effect of the misery thoughts on your friendships, family, work, hopes for the future?*

- *Are there times or places when the misery thoughts have more influence?*

- *Are there times or places where they have less influence or not so much influence?*

- *Has the effect of the misery thoughts changed over time?*

- *Are there any warning signs that the misery thoughts are coming?*

Each of these questions can be a site for further enquiry. For example, if the effects have been less at work or when with her family, I might want to enquire about what Antje understood was contributing to this lessening of the effects. I might ask questions about whether there were particular things that Antje was doing in these situations, or whether she had ideas/thoughts that were more readily available to her at those times that stood against 'the misery thoughts', or whether there were particular people or environments that she found supportive of her on these occasions.

In asking these sorts of questions I was able to hear from Antje about the actions that she was already taking whenever these 'misery thoughts' were coming into her thinking. I heard about how Antje had learned to recognise these thoughts as distinct from other thoughts. I learned about what Antje does to care for and protect herself from the ploys of these thoughts. And I learnt about the people in her life who would know about her struggle with these thoughts and who want to see her succeed in banishing them from her life.

A thorough mapping of the effects of the problem often creates space for the articulation of these solution knowledges and the intentions and hopes. Again, it is important that the mapping of effects is detailed and thorough and that I do not quickly rush into these openings into preferred stories. The abuse has often had pervasive effects on the lives of the women who consult with me.

Mapping the effects of the externalised problem is a way of acknowledging these effects, and at the same time creating openings that can be explored later.

Putting stage one and stage two together – Janet's story[5]

Janet sought counselling when she was 46 years old. When we first met she was barely able to find her voice. She spoke very quietly and tentatively. Over time I heard about her experience of sexual abuse and neglect as a child. I heard about how she was removed from her family and about the loss of her relationship with her mother due to domestic violence. Throughout these conversations I also heard of her own commitments in relation to her two adult children, about pride she had in her own abilities as a parent, and about her love for her children. The hopes and dreams that she had for herself were also shared.

During the times of our talking together, one of the significant turning points for Janet was a conversation in which she renamed what had earlier been described by a previous counsellor as 'social phobia'. Janet told me that she had had her doubts about the term 'social phobia'. She knew that what she was experiencing was due to the abuse she had experienced. She thought that the description 'social phobia' didn't quite fit for her although she could see why someone else might think it did. We spent some time considering some possible names for what she was experiencing and Janet mentioned the metaphor of a 'safe spot'. Janet had come across this description in some reading that she had been doing and the idea of 'the safe spot' seemed to provide a good fit for her. Exploring the effect and influence of 'the safe spot' in Janet's life became a key theme in many further conversations.

In these conversations we were able to consider the effects of 'the safe spot' on a number of aspects of Janet's life: on her relationships with friends, on her ability to socialise in the way that she wanted to, on her work, and on how she saw herself. I heard how 'the safe spot' wanted Janet to be 'far away from the focus of attention' where she would not be noticed. When she walked into a room, 'the safe spot' had Janet watching for the place she could sit that would feel most safe, e.g. near the door/behind a table/in the kitchen on the other side of the bench. It had her constantly thinking about who she would feel safest sitting next to and how she would move around a room if she needed to. 'The safe spot' would also want her to plan carefully for any times that she left her flat, and led her to be highly watchful when out in the streets shopping or walking. I heard about how 'the safe spot' had also made it hard for Janet to socialise and that it was sensitive to any signs of abruptness from others. 'The safe spot' often stopped Janet from saying what she didn't like and stopped her from forming friendships. These things were all having a big effect on Janet's life.

I was curious about the history of 'the safe spot' and wondered if it had always been around in Janet's life – had it always been so influential or had there been times when it wasn't around or was less around? It was in asking about this history that I was able to hear from Janet about how important achieving safety had been in her life. I came to hear about how the effects of 'the safe spot' were not solely negative. In fact, there was a history of 'the safe spot' looking after Janet and her sister. I heard about this history of how 'the safe spot' had engaged Janet in: practices of watchfulness for her own safety and that of her sister; practices of careful attentiveness to the mood of her father; practices of cleverness as a child in finding different hiding places in the house from which she could watch with safety; practices of skilful negotiation with bullying boys at school; practices of seeking sanctuary in the bush within which she hid to keep safe at school; and practices of escape through which Janet, at the times of the abuse, had been able to take herself away, in her thinking, to a place of safety.

What also emerged in these conversations was an account of the context of abuse in which 'the safe spot' had developed. I heard about how other adults and organisations had often let Janet and her sister down in relation to matters of safety and care. The conversations that were shared made visible the conditions in which the negative and constraining stories Janet had of herself had been created.

These conversations enabled Janet to review the effects of abuse, and she described this review as 'like walking out from behind a brick wall'. Having moved away from calling the problem 'social phobia' and exploring an understanding of 'the safe spot' and its effects in her life, Janet then made some further discernments. Janet decided that the negative effects of 'the safe spot' were actually due to 'the voice of abuse'. This new naming created further space for Janet to renegotiate the meaning she had given to her experiences of abuse. It also enabled her to notice the influence of relations of class and gender in the bullying at school. Through these conversations Janet was able to acknowledge the injustice of what she had been through and to experience outrage and anger at her father's abuse and neglect of her and her brothers and sisters when they were children. She was also able to name her father's continued claims to entitlement, and his pretence that everything was okay and that nothing had happened. In time, Janet was able to make a stand against her father's denial of the truth of what happened to her as a child and this was very significant to her.

I would like to briefly recount how the first two stages of the 'Statement of position map' informed my thinking in relation to this story of Janet's experience. Janet came to counselling with a negative and constraining description of herself that had been developed in a context of abuse. Through the conversations we shared, she was able to name the problem in a way that did not describe her as having 'social phobia' but instead named the problem in her terms as 'the safe spot'. This externalised definition of the problem enabled her to explore the effects 'the safe spot' was having in her life. Through this exploration of the effects of the problem, Janet was also able to identify and describe the context in which 'the safe spot' had developed. Identifying this context enabled Janet to name the silencing and the claims to entitlement that had contributed to the development of the negative stories she had of her life. It also enabled her to develop different meanings that challenged these old stories.

Stage three: *Evaluation of the effects*

The third stage of the 'Statement of position map' involves inviting the person to evaluate the effects of the problem. When I first began to work with the practices of narrative therapy, it was this idea of inviting the person consulting with me to evaluate the effects of the problem that surprised me the most. In hindsight, the surprise that I felt was due to unspoken assumptions on my part. I was accustomed to making assumptions about the effects of certain events and ideas on people's lives, and yet these assumptions can obscure the intentions, purposes, beliefs and hopes of those who consult with us.

In seeking an evaluation of the effects of the problem, I am engaged in a practice of decentering myself as therapist/counsellor and inviting the women to take a position in relation to the effects of the abuse.

In talking with Antje, for example, about the effects of 'the misery thoughts', I might have asked questions like:

- 'So would you say that "the misery thoughts" have been useful or not so useful in your life?'

- 'Is it okay or not for "the misery thoughts" to have this kind of say in your friendships?'

- 'This might seem like an obvious question, but I wanted to check if "the misery thoughts" have been a good or bad thing or maybe something else?'

- 'Would you want more or less of "the misery thoughts" in your life?'

These kinds of questions also privilege ideas of choice. For example, to think about whether she wants 'the misery thoughts' to continue to have such a say in her life, Antje is able to experience her own agency in relation to the effects of the problem. These questions provide further opportunity to identify the operations and effects of the problem, and for her to separate herself from these.

This evaluative enquiry is not simply about resolving that something is either okay or not okay, good or bad. Frequently, evaluative questions lead to the articulation of complexity and specificity. For example, Janet might conclude that 'the safe spot' was helpful in her childhood in protecting her from further abuse, but that many of its effects in the present are not good – for example, the way it is talking her out of friendships.

This practice of asking women about their evaluation of the effects of the problem recognises their special knowledge about what suits them in their own life. Often this stands so strongly in contrast to these women's previous experiences. Many women who have experienced child sexual abuse have had their bodies, voices and beliefs disregarded and violated. In the years after the abuse they have often been silenced and disbelieved. For therapists to remain de-centered and to ask women to evaluate, in detail, the effects of the problem, recognises and acknowledges women's knowledge and expertise in relation to their own life. It also creates opportunities for therapists to hear more about the intentions, beliefs, values, purposes that women have for their lives.

Stage four: *Justification of the evaluation*

In the final stage, I ask women to justify their evaluation of the effects of the problem. 'Why would you determine this effect of the problem in your life positive/ negative?' 'Why is it that you would say that this effect is not okay in your life?' Asking these questions is often a joyful experience for me in this work because in asking women why they would take a particular position on the problem opens space for them to speak about the values and commitments that they hold.

For example, Antje said to me that it was not okay for misery to have the effects it does in her life because it takes her away from being with her children in the way that she wants to be with them. Another woman might state that the reason she believes the effects of the problem are negative is because they stop her having fun, or stop her from working, or prevent her getting an education which they have always wanted, or block her enjoyment of friendships. Alternatively, a woman might say that the reason she believes that the effects are negative is because she doesn't believe anyone should experience what she is experiencing. In hearing about these justifications, I am then able to ask further questions that unearth the histories of these aspects of women's lives – histories of desires for friendship, fun, work, and so on. These are stories and histories that have often been obscured by the effects of the abuse but have nonetheless remained treasured and cherished.

To refrain from asking for a justification of the evaluation, to not ask 'why?', is to miss opportunities to invite people to speak to important commitments that stand against the effect of abuse in their lives. These justifications of the evaluations provide many openings for re-authoring conversations.[6]

To conclude let me offer an example of asking for an evaluation of the effects of the problem and then for a justification of this evaluation. Julie surprised me recently when she said that her experience of standing up to the voice of abuse was bad for her. I had expected her to be pleased with the action she had taken in being clear about what she wanted in a difficult situation and so I was curious about how this was a bad thing for her. In inviting Julie to justify her evaluation I was able to hear about how in standing up for herself she had used language that she would have preferred not to, and about how she had shouted. For Julie, this was a significant disappointment. In speaking in the way that she did, she felt she had behaved no better than her father who had abused her as a child, and she believed she was better than that. Julie had strong beliefs about the ways she preferred to speak to people, even when she disagreed with them. These ways of speaking valued respect and kindness above abusive ways. What followed from this was a larger discussion about why she didn't like yelling and a thickening up of why she preferred more respectful ways. We explored what it said about Julie that she was deliberately creating a life in which she upheld values of respect and kindness. Julie also stated that she valued her regret and remorse about yelling, as this distinguished her from those who are abusive and who do not seem to feel such remorse or regret.

Conclusion

In the first part of this paper I have tried to describe how the 'Statement of position map' shapes my conversations with women who have survived child sexual abuse. The practices embodied in this map remind me of my intentions to provide a listening space that makes it more possible for women to speak out and act against the effects of child sexual abuse in their lives. This is not a linear process. Even when conversations are shaped by such a map, these do not proceed in a linear fashion. Conversations do not move neatly from 'externalising the problem' to 'mapping the effects' to 'evaluation' and 'justification', but weave to and fro through all the aspects of the map. The journey of this work is creative. There are stops and starts, moments where we might feel as though there has not been much movement, times when we feel stuck and the questions don't come easily. And then there are other times, when women such as Antje, Janet, Natalie and Julie begin to reclaim their lives from the effects of abuse and richly describe their own knowledges, hopes, values and dreams.

Part II: Definitional ceremony and outsider-witnessing

by
Shona Russell

When we meet women in counselling we often hear stories about the significance of other people. People who are friends, partners, family members, extended family, grandmothers, and so on, frequently hold a place of importance in the lives of those who consult us. There are many ways of bringing the thoughts, ideas and voices of these people into the counselling process, and in this paper I will focus on how outsider-witness practices and definitional ceremonies can enable others to play a part in joining with women who are reclaiming their lives from the effects of child sexual abuse.

A feature of narrative therapy has been to create processes whereby audience members act as witnesses, in very particular ways, to the conversation between the therapist and those coming for therapy (see Morgan 2000, p.121).

The work of a cultural anthropologist, Barbara Myerhoff (1986), and in particular her description of *definitional ceremonies*, has been introduced into therapeutic contexts by Michael White (1995b). These definitional ceremonies are carefully structured events in which an audience of people witness the stories told by the person consulting the therapist and then respond in considered ways.

The people who are invited to participate as an audience in these definitional ceremonies are often referred to as 'outsider-witnesses'. These people who agree to act as witnesses may be family members, partners, friends, people who are members of a small community or group, or a group of professional counsellors.[7]

Definitional ceremonies are made up of four stages:

The stages of definitional ceremonies

1. Re-authoring conversation

This first part involves the outsider witnesses listening to the therapeutic conversation between the therapist and the person who has come for therapy. This conversation seeks to open space for the articulation of unique outcomes and preferred stories.

2. Outsider-witness re-telling

Outsider-witness members change places with the person being interviewed and the therapist. The family/individual and therapist now listen as the outsider-witness group engages in a re-telling of what they have heard. The retelling conversation is guided by practices of narrative therapy that keep responses de-centered in form (see White 1995b, 1997, 1999 for full descriptions of the principles that inform outsider-witness responses).

3. Response to the Re-telling

The outsider witnesses once again swap places with the therapist and the person who was initially interviewed. The third part of the process involves the family/ individual commenting on the re-tellings of the outsider-witness group. This happens by the therapist asking: 'What most interested you about the group comments? Why? What stands out most from what you heard?'. In this way persons re-engage with unique outcomes or aspects of their preferred, alternative story, and are able to experience these more richly.

4. Discussion of the Therapy

The last part of the process involves asking the outsider–witness group to join the family/individual and the therapist for a discussion in which everyone involved reflects on the process. In this stage the therapist is often asked questions about their contribution to the initial re-authoring conversation. The therapist may also ask the outsider-witness group about their re-tellings. Family members choose whether or not join in this discussion which is linked to narrative practices of transparency.

Within this four stage process, what matters most is the ability of the outsider-witness participants to do more than summarise what they have heard. Outsider-witness practices provide an opportunity for preferred stories to be acknowledged, confirmed and expanded through re-tellings. The task of outsider witnesses is to go beyond or exceed the boundaries of the first telling. By reflecting on the initial telling, and describing how what they heard will influence their own understandings of life and work, the re-tellings of the outsider witnesses provide space for significant aspects of life that are often dismissed or ignored, to be noticed and inquired about. In these ways, outsider-witness members act as an audience to the *performance* of preferred identity descriptions. This process is often described as 'thickening' preferred identity claims. Barbara Myerhoff (1986) in describing the ways in which elderly Jewish residents of a community centre deliberately created ceremonies which defined and re-defined their identities in ways in which they preferred, emphasised the metaphor of performance:

> ... *definitional ceremonies provide opportunities for being seen and in one's own terms, garnering witnesses to one's own worth, vitality and being. Thus, it was the custom for Centre members to display and dramatize themselves in many forms, informal and formal, planned and spontaneously storytelling, creating difficulties, making scenes; by positioning themselves to be noticed, recorded, listened to, and photographed. Definitional ceremonies were the elders' most regular and formal patterns of display, and it was the performative dimension of definitional ceremonies that was the critical ingredient ... (p.267)*

Child sexual abuse

There are particular aspects of my work with women who have been subjected to child sexual abuse that contribute to my interest in therapeutic definitional ceremony work. In my experience, when women request counselling for the effects of child sexual abuse they often come with very negative and self-destructive accounts of themselves. The abuse has powerfully influenced the stories the women have about their lives, and in turn these stories provide the frame through which people interpret their experiences of life.

The conditions that enable child sexual abuse to occur include the imbalance in relationships of power between adults and children, and the tactics of fear, trickery and confusion that enforce and maintain silence about the child sexual abuse. Because of this silence, the negative and self-destructive stories of life that have been shaped by abuse often remain unchallenged for many years. In the conversations I have with women I frequently hear how they, as children, wanted the abuse to stop. I also hear descriptions of actions, often very creative and ingenious actions, that the women took as children to try to escape or to stop the abuse from happening. Frequently, however, there has not been an audience or witness to these alternative accounts of life or to the preferred wishes and intentions of the women. Neither has there been an audience which identifies and names the abuse as injustice, exploitation and/or torture. In the absence of witnesses to these alternative accounts of identity, it can be very difficult to renegotiate the dominant negative self descriptions that have been shaped by the abuse. In recognising that identity is a social achievement, it is therefore necessary to provide forums in which the renegotiation of the meanings that shape identity are witnessed and authenticated by others.

There are a number of ways in which people can break from the very negative stories and descriptions of identity that are commonly the effects of abuse. Definitional ceremonies and outsider-witness practices have an important role to play in such achievements by providing a structure for developing alternative accounts of the experiences of abuse and alternative stories of life. Another way of describing this is to say that structured forums can provide a space and experience which authenticates (confirms, validates) what people hope for in their lives, and also what they know about their lives.

A group for young women who had experienced child sexual abuse

To convey an account of the ways in which definitional ceremonies can be utilised in work with survivors of child sexual abuse, I will now describe the work of a group for young women survivors. The idea for offering a group program within the counselling service came from a discussion with a colleague, Michelle Cherubin. We wanted to provide a therapeutic response that offered possibilities for shared conversations and that would contribute to a sense of connection between young women who had identified child sexual abuse as the primary reason for their referral to the service. A number of young women were attending individual counselling and during conversations with them it had become clear that they wanted to know about the ideas and experiences of other young women.

Coming together - what does it stand for?

We also wanted to provide a response that would challenge the dominant cultural practice of individualising problems and, in turn, lessen the isolation that was being experienced by the young women. Many of the young women described effects of child sexual abuse in terms of experiences of guilt, shame and fear. We thought that shared conversations may open different possibilities for undermining such effects. We also suspected that young women together might have quite a lot to say about the cultural and gender specifications to which they were subjected.

As our work is grounded in the understanding that life and identity is a social project, we speculated that young women together could have quite an impact on shaping each other's identity descriptions in ways that were linked to the hopes they had for their own lives, rather than to the negative conclusions resulting from experiences of abuse. We hoped that engaging the young women in re-authoring conversations, while other young women acted as an audience to witness and acknowledge preferred identity claims, would offer new possibilities for the development of alternative stories of the young women's lives.

A number of young women were keen to meet together and an eight week group was started for women aged from 14-18 years old. We focused on this particular group because at that time there were no other group services available for young women of these ages.

Before discussing some of the work of the group, I would like to paint a picture of the lives of these young women. In the group there were five young women who came from a range of backgrounds and who were involved in many activities including school, computer graphics, filmmaking, and tertiary studies. Their living arrangements varied and for some included the risk of homelessness, while others lived with family members. The young women were very interested to find out about each others' lives – they were interested in where the others were living and wanted to hear about each other's achievements and plans for their futures. The initial sharing of these stories held special significance for the group as hearing about each other's achievements and hopes formed a rich and full account of the lives of each young woman. These preferred descriptions of life contrasted with the limited identity descriptions encouraged by the effects of abuse. The group was structured in ways that ensured that these preferred stories of life were privileged in all the meetings that were held. It was while standing in these alternative territories that the young women were more able to share stories about how experiences of abuse were continuing to affect their experience of themselves and their lives – experiences that at times led to self-harm, self-hate, doubt and fear.

Speaking out

During the second week of the group one of the young women, who I shall call Beth, said she wanted to tell the others about what had happened to her. I would like to describe in some detail our response to this request, the ideas informing our response, and the action that followed.

In preparing the young women for the group, we had been clear that speaking about specific experiences of abuse was not a requirement of the group and would not be asked of group members. This view reflects the belief that it is not necessary to revisit or describe the events that led up to abuse, or what happened during the assault or immediately after, in order to reduce the effects of abuse and to re-author one's experiences. Many people attending counselling have told me that they expect to be asked to repeat stories of the particularities of the abuse, and for many people this idea evokes considerable fear and dread. Such practices can inadvertently reconnect survivors with the experience of trauma, and can indeed re-traumatise. Requiring survivors to recall and re-tell the experiences of abuse is likely to reinforce the very meanings that were constructed at the time of the abuse. As these meanings were constructed in circumstances and conditions in which the child had little or no control over the situation, and in which there was a gross imbalance of power, to encourage a re-visiting of the events of abuse often ignores the politics of abuse and contributes to an escalation of trauma and distress. This was not the intention of the group.

However, we did have some ideas about ways of responding to Beth's request – responses that we hoped would provide Beth with the kind of audience she had not had before, that would contribute to a different expression of her experiences of abuse, and that would place Beth's experience in context in ways that acknowledged the politics of abuse. This involved using the definitional ceremony structure outlined above.

Preparing for the definitional ceremony

Before we held the definitional ceremony there was considerable preparation to do. We began by holding a private conversation with Beth. Rather than interviewing her about the specifics of the abuse she had been subjected to, we instead interviewed her about her interest in speaking out and about what she was expecting this might be like.

This conversation shed light on important aspects of Beth's experience. Beth had told some friends at school about the abuse and this had not gone well. When Beth had spoken to these friends she experienced being disbelieved and disapproved of – she had felt degraded. She told us that her friends really didn't know what to do or say and that she felt worse after she told them. As a result of that disclosure at school Beth had felt silenced for a long time. Beth said she liked the others in this therapeutic group and that she thought that speaking with them would be different than her experience at school.

We also spoke with Beth about the commonly held idea that speaking about abuse or disclosing abuse can be seen as necessary for recovery. We wanted to check Beth's ideas about this and she was clear that she wanted to talk in the group because she believed it would be different to her previous experience. This would mean a lot to her.

Michelle and I agreed to go ahead with this because we also thought the young women would offer a response which would be honouring of Beth, and would demonstrate belief, understanding and care. Further than this, we thought it would be possible to create a context which would powerfully authenticate the knowledges, skills and hopes that Beth had about her own life. This would be a very significant opportunity for a different experience for Beth.

Because we were not prepared to leave the response to Beth's retelling to chance, we sought agreement from the group about a process we believed could contribute to honouring Beth's story. We would invite Beth to speak about aspects of her story in response to questions we would ask, and invite other group members to listen to the conversation. The group members would act as witnesses to the conversation and then would be asked to speak about their experience of listening.

Preparing outsider witnesses is an important part of the process. To be an audience to people's life stories is important and we took time to discuss a number of taken-for-granted ideas which can influence the ways people offer reflections. For example, it is common for witnesses to offer advice or solutions to the person who has just offered their stories, e.g. 'What worked really well for me was ...', or 'I think the best thing you could do is ...'. While this advice is generally offered with good intention and in kind ways, these are not the sort of reflections that we are looking for in outsider-witness work. The intention of re-authoring conversations is to connect the person at the centre of the definitional ceremony (in this situation Beth) with the ideas and knowledges that they have about their own life, and to their skills. Offering advice from the outside is not the aim of the process. The other common response by people new to the process can be to go off on a tangent with their reflections, one that moves the discussion too far away from the person who is at the centre of the process (in this situation Beth). Knowing that these are the sorts of hazards that can accompany outsider-witness work, it was important for us to provide a context for the process of listening and responding to Beth. We worked to create a witnessing context which would focus on aspects of life that Beth had identified as significant to her.

We did this by asking the group if they would be interested in forming a 'listening group' to firstly listen and hear Beth's story and then respond to what they had heard. We explained that there were several steps which could guide the work of the listening group:

1. To acknowledge what Beth had said. In other words to say something to honour the significance of Beth's story. This step is very important to create a listening space of respect, care and acknowledgement for what has been spoken about. This makes a big difference in terms of ensuring that the re-telling is re-grading of Beth's life.

2. To notice what it was like to hear the conversation. In other words to say something about the ways you have been touched or moved by listening to what Beth spoke about.

3. To say why you were touched or moved by certain things that Beth said and how this is linked to your own life.

4. To comment on the ways this conversation will have effects on your own life – what you now might think differently about, what you might do differently from now on.

The young women were eager to participate in these ways so we then provided some questions as a guide for their reflections. These included:

1. What has it been like for you to hear Beth's story?

2. What stands out to you as you listened? Can you say something about why this stands out to you?

3. Did any of the things Beth said have you thinking differently about your own life? In what ways?

In previous discussions some of the young women had talked about how they wished to find ways of dealing with the considerable anger that they felt about the issue of sexual assault. Some of the young women in the group had, in the past, been recruited into self-harming, particularly cutting, which they had described as a consequence of their anger and outrage. In response to this we formed a particular question:

4. If you have noticed being angry about things in response to listening to Beth, what options might there be for responding to the sort of injustice that she has been describing?

After Beth had spoken, the group offered their reflections based on these questions and then Beth was asked what it was like to hear from the listening team. When Beth spoke about what stood out for her in the group's re-telling, and what she would like to think more about, she had a clearer sense of what she wanted for her life.

For Beth, the conversations and comments of the listening team contributed to a very different experience of speaking about abuse. The re-telling offered descriptions of Beth that focused on the abilities, skills and the hopes she had for her life. Throughout the process these descriptions were offered in different ways. Each of the young women found ways of being very loving and caring towards Beth and towards each other. Such expressions contradicted some of the ideas about being permanently damaged by experiences of abuse and also provided a context for safe expressions of anger, outrage, hurt and sadness. The kindness and caring also enabled expressions of laughter and the sharing of re-grading stories.

Conversations of deconstruction

Some of the reflections paved the way for discussion about the broader factors that make it difficult to speak about abuse. The group had the following things to say about why they found it hard to speak about their experiences of abuse:

- *We're afraid people won't believe us.*
- *If you speak out something else will happen.*
- *I don't know what to say, or how to say it.*
- *I worry what people might say.*
- *Before telling, you can pretend it didn't happen.*
- *It's embarrassing.*
- *We worry about getting people into trouble.*
- *We worry about being a burden to others.*
- *We don't want to hurt others.*

The responses listed here provide an account of the significant impact that dominant ideas in relation to the sexual abuse have on young women's lives. Narrative practices provide a framework for the ongoing review and questioning (deconstruction) of strongly held beliefs that have an impact on the construction of identity.

After the young women had spoken about why they find it hard to talk about experiences of abuse, Michelle and I then offered our own outsider-witness reflection about the origin of ideas such as 'it's my fault', or 'you provoked it'. This led to asking the group the following questions:

- Where do you think these ideas have come from?
- How do you think these ideas impact on the lives of women and girls?
- Who do these ideas most benefit?

The discussion which followed was critical in beginning to interrupt very powerful messages and beliefs that had captured the young women and which contributed to some of the negative and damming accounts the young women had of their identities. Our intention was to open discussion that named and identified dominant discourses. Identifying practices of power that maintained gender discourses began to open space for young women to question previously held ideas such as 'it is your fault', 'you asked for it' and 'you could have stopped him/her'.

Most significantly, this discussion occurred within a group, not in isolation, and this contributed to a shared connection for group members in their stand against the effects of abuse. We acknowledged the stand that the young women were taking in coming along to the group and asked them to consider what they may have been standing up to and what they were standing for. They said:

- *I am resisting blame.*
- *I am standing up for my own beliefs and experiences.*
- *To be with others is what I believe in.*
- *I'm standing for trusting what I'm feeling and thinking it's okay.*
- *I am standing for fairness.*
- *I'm standing for creating trusting relationships.*
- *To rebuild trust and be safe – that's what I am standing for.*

As illustrated by the statements in relation to '*being with others*', '*creating trusting relationships*' and '*being safe*', the group was providing a forum where the young women could join with each other in their stand against sexual abuse. The group was also a place where the young women together were building relationships with each other based on honesty, care and safety.

A final ceremony

In planning for this young women's group, Michelle and I spoke about the ways we wanted to make space for the skills, knowledges and experiences that the young women brought with them to shape and influence the group process. One example involved planning for the final group meeting.

As we approached the final week (week eight) many of the young women expressed disappointment about the group finishing and they were keen for the final meeting to be something special. They talked about how much getting to know each other had meant to them and we had noticed the many ways they had contributed to each other's lives.

We recognised that the final group meeting had the potential to be a powerful marker in the lives of the young women and wished to create a ceremony to enable this. The group had been together for eight weeks and during that time had been very active in pursuing particular identity projects that connected them with preferred descriptions of their lives. The ceremony was to act as an acknowledgement and recognition of the shifts in identity descriptions that had developed through the interactions between group members. We hoped this ceremony would highlight and strengthen the connections made, the stories told, and the ideas that had been discussed. Myerhoff's words (1986) seemed particularly appropriate. This was an opportunity for the young women to be ... *seen in one's own terms, garnering witnesses to one's own worth, vitality and being* (p.267).

The planning of this last session was done in consultation with all the group members. It was decided that different activities would be included with the intention of more fully and richly describing the preferred identities of each group member. The gathering was to be held in a beautiful place and the Botanic Gardens in the city centre was chosen. Everyone was to bring a favourite food of some kind to share. The young women really wanted to bring gifts and this was organised by drawing names out of a hat. The gift was to be inexpensive and what mattered was to say something within the ceremony about the significance of the gift.

It was also decided that each person would say something about what being in the group had meant to them. These words would then be written up as a document, copies of which would be posted out to each young woman. Finally, the young women wanted to have a group photograph taken which would be posted out with the document.

As we arrived in the city gardens laden with food, gifts, camera, paper and pens, I was mindful of how different this experience was to the first meeting of the group eight weeks ago. At that time, embarrassment, shame, tentativeness, rage, fear, isolation, as well as the initial steps in taking a stand against the effects of sexual abuse, were all very present. The experience and energy in the city gardens was very different. I remember noticing how the young women were so loving and caring towards each other, the ways they were connecting, and how they contributed to describing each other's lives in hopeful and encouraging ways. The abilities they had to listen to each other and respond in heartfelt ways were very obvious on that day, and most of all I remember their laughter.

We all went through the steps of the ceremony which we had planned together. We ate together, we shared gifts, we spoke about these gifts, we talked about what it had meant to be a part of this group, and we documented the words of the group members before taking the group photograph.

This is what group members said about what the group had meant to them:

- *The group has been a thing of security. I knew if I wanted to say something the rest of the group wouldn't laugh. Instead they would support me in what I wanted to say.*

- *This group has meant a lot to me because when I first came I didn't know anyone who had been through what I had been through. I didn't know what others felt like. Now I do know and I really like that.*

- *This group has been a safe place where I can come and be totally accepted for who I am and the experiences I have been through.*

- *I think the group has offered a sense of security. I have been able to talk openly and everyone else has told the truth. We are all survivors who have been able to come here together and that's good. Everyone has been there for each other. We can go anywhere in life if we want it bad enough. We can do what we want, not what anyone else wants.*

- *The group has shown me that I can be who I want. It has been great to hear other stories of people's survival and this has helped me in my journey. It has been great to get to know so many wonderful people.*

Summary

In this paper we (SM and SR) have tried to convey how we are engaging with particular narrative practices in our conversations with women survivors of child sexual abuse. This paper has focused on the use of the 'Statement of position map' and the use of 'outsider-witness practices' and 'definitional ceremonies'. This paper does not represent a full account of therapy with women in relation to child sexual abuse. We simply hope that it offers a realistic depiction of some aspects of our work and conveys a sense of the part that these practices play in making possible the acknowledgement and rich description of the knowledges, skills, hopes and dreams of those women and young women with whom we work.

Acknowledgement

This paper reflects an ongoing commitment from the child sexual abuse counselling team at Adelaide Central Mission, South Australia, to collaborative, decentred practices in our work with men and women who have been subjected to sexual abuse. We want to acknowledge and honour the lives of the women whose experiences and contributions influence the ideas discussed here.

Many people have contributed to the commitments and ideas in our work. We would particularly like to acknowledge past and present members of the Adelaide Central Mission Family Services and the Child Sexual Abuse Team.

Notes

This paper was originally published in the *International Journal of Narrative Therapy & Community Work*, 2002 No.3. Republished here with permission.

1. Sue Mann is a member of the Dulwich Centre Teaching Faculty and is a counsellor at the Adelaide Central Mission in the Child Sexual Abuse Team where she can be contacted c/o 10 Pitt St, Adelaide 5000, South Australia, or via email: counsel@acm.asn.au   Shona Russell is also a member of the Dulwich Centre Teaching Faculty where she also works as a counsellor. Shona can be contacted c/o Dulwich Centre Publications, or via email: swrussell@bigpond.com

2. For other descriptions of the use of narrative practices in relation to work with the survivors of child sexual abuse see Kamsler (1990), White (1995a), Silent Too Long Inc. (2000),Linnell & Cora (1993), Bird (2000), Jenkins, Joy & Hall (2002). For other

descriptions about the effects and politics of child sexual abuse see Breckenridge & Laing (1999), Verco (2002). For broader descriptions of the influence of sexism, heterosexism and racism on women's lives see Lorde (1984).

3. For further discussion of externalising problems see Carey & Russell (2002).

4. For further descriptions of the experience of survivors consulting therapists see Silent Too Long Inc. (2000).

5. Although I have chosen to use this story of Janet's to illustrate the first two stages of the 'Statement of position map', it seems important to note that all four stages of the map were woven throughout our conversations.

6. Once these openings are articulated it is possible to engage in further re-authoring conversations, re-membering conversations and other forms of conversation that enable preferred stories to become more richly described. See Morgan (2000) for further information about steps that can then be taken with these conversations.

7. For example, when working with a young woman, Maria, who had been sexually assaulted by her uncle as a child, after several meetings it became clear that the effects of this abuse had driven a wedge between Maria, her sister and her mother. Maria wanted her mother and sister to join with her in reconnecting with them and we invited them to be part of the counselling processes and to act as witnesses to the changes Maria was hoping for. In this instance Maria's sister and mother acted as outsider witnesses.

References

Bird, J. 2000: *The Heart's Narrative*. Auckland: Edge Press.

Breckenridge J.& Laing, L. (eds). 1999: *Breaking Silence*. Sydney: Allen & Unwin.

Burr, V. 1995: *An Introduction to Social Constructionism*. London: Routledge.

Carey, M. & Russell S. 2002: 'Externalising: Commonly asked questions.' *The International Journal of Narrative Therapy and Community Work*, No.2.

Jenkins, A., Joy, M. & Hall, R. 2002: 'Forgiveness and child sexual abuse: A matrix of meanings.' *The International Journal of Narrative Therapy and Community Work*, No.1.

Joy, M. 1999: 'Shame on who? Consulting with children who have experienced sexual abuse.' In Morgan, A. (ed): *Once Upon a Time ... Narrative therapy with children and their families*. Adelaide: Dulwich Centre Publications.

Kamsler, A. 1990: 'Her-story in the making: Therapy with women who were sexually abused in childhood.' In Durrant, M. & White, C. (eds): *Ideas for Therapy with Sexual Abuse*. Adelaide: Dulwich Centre Publications. Reprinted 1998 in White, C. & Denborough D. (eds): *Introducing Narrative Therapy: A collection of practice-based writings*. Adelaide: Dulwich Centre Publications.

Linnell, S. & Cora, D. 1993: *Discoveries: A group resource guide for women who have been sexually abused in childhood.* Sydney: Dympna House.

Lorde, A. 1984: *Sister Outsider: Essays and speeches.* California: The Crossing Press.

Morgan, A. 2000: *What is Narrative Therapy? An easy-to-read introduction.* Adelaide: Dulwich Centre Publications.

Myerhoff, B. 1986: 'Life not death in Venice; Its second life'. In Turner, V. & Bruner, E. (eds): *The Anthropology of Experience.* Chicago: University of Illinois Press.

Myerhoff, B. 1982: 'Life history among the elderly: Performance, visibility and re-membering' in Ruby, J. (ed): *A Crack in the Mirror. Reflective perspectives in Anthropology.* Philadelphia: University of Pennsylvania Press.

O'Leary, P. 1998: 'Liberation from self-blame: Working with men who have experienced childhood sexual abuse.' *Dulwich Centre Journal,* No.4. Reprinted 1999 in: *Extending Narrative Therapy.* Adelaide: Dulwich Centre Publications.

Silent Too Long Inc. 2000: 'Embracing the old, nurturing the new.' *Dulwich Centre Journal,* Nos. 1 & 2.

Verco, J. 2002: 'Women's outrage and the pressure to forgive.' *The International Journal of Narrative Therapy and Community Work,* No.1.

White, M. 1995a: 'Naming abuse and breaking from its effects.' In White, M.: *Re-Authoring Lives: Interviews and essays.* Adelaide: Dulwich Centre Publications.

White, M. 1995b: 'Reflecting teamwork as definitional ceremony.' In White, M.: *Re-Authoring Lives: Interviews and essays.* Adelaide: Dulwich Centre Publications.

White, M. 1997: *Narratives of Therapists' Lives.* Adelaide: Dulwich Centre Publications.

White, 1999: 'Reflecting teamwork as definitional ceremony revisited.' *Gecko: a journal of deconstruction and narrative ideas in therapeutic practice,* Vol 1. Reprinted in White, M. 2000: *Reflections on Narrative Practice: Essays and interviews.* Adelaide: Dulwich Centre Publications.

White, M. 2002: Workshop notes published on Dulwich Centre Website: www.dulwichcentre.com.au/articles/mwworkshopnotes

2.

Forgiveness and child sexual abuse

A matrix of meanings

by

Alan Jenkins, Rob Hall &
Maxine Joy[1]

The concept of forgiveness, along with notions of apology and atonement for wrongs, can constitute highly significant preoccupations for individuals and communities whose lives have been affected by abuse. People who have been abused, those who have acted abusively and members of their families and broader communities may all have concerns and hopes about forgiveness and atonement. In the aftermath of sexual abuse, concerns about forgiveness may range from, 'I'll never forgive' to 'Why can't I forgive?' and these concerns may be met with preoccupations like, 'I've said I'm sorry, surely it's time for her to forgive me' and 'You must learn to forgive and forget'.

Concerns and dilemmas about forgiveness are extremely wide-ranging and pervasive, perhaps because it is so frequently highlighted as an important virtue in most spiritual and secular philosophies, from traditional to new age.

Alexander Pope is credited with the influential maxim, 'To err is human to forgive divine'. Popular commentator, Stephanie Dowrick, has regarded forgiveness as transcendental or, 'the supreme virtue, the most virtuous of virtues, the apotheosis of love' (Dowrick 1997).

As virtues, the concepts of forgiveness and atonement can be inspirational. They highlight notions of choice as opposed to pathology and inevitability. Despite the levels of betrayal, harm and humiliation brought about by abuse, there is the possibility of release from suffering for the abused person. There are also the possibilities of remorse, responsibility, restitution and redemption for the person who has abused. These possibilities are extended to the communities in which these individuals live. Such options are proposed as possible and achievable choices.

However, the same concepts can be equally oppressive when they become experienced as mandatory obligations rather than possibilities and choices. Both forgiveness and atonement can relate to realisations which are freely made or to requirements and expectations which are enforced by judgemental ideologies and oppressive practices.

Notions of forgiveness and atonement can have many meanings for different individuals who have experienced abuse. A range of popular meanings inform the nature of possibilities and choices available to individuals and communities, as well as expectations and demands made by others. Meanings are often confused and conflicting, leading to dilemmas which hinder respectful outcomes, when attempts are made to address experiences of abusive behaviour.

We have attempted to deconstruct popular meanings associated with the concepts of forgiveness and atonement, in order to enable the drawing of distinctions between the range of concepts and ideas which are commonly used. This process can be helpful in informing respectful choices. To this end, we have compiled a matrix of popular meanings which may be helpful in making sense of the 'journeys of realisation', undertaken both by those who have been abused and by those who have perpetrated abuse.

Popular meanings of forgiveness

There appear to be three major components of meaning in popular constructs of forgiveness, in relation to the experiences of those who have been subjected to abuse:

1. **relinquishment**: this component refers to notions of acceptance and letting go of undesired feelings and ideas. In popular concepts, particular emphasis is placed on:
   - a lessening or cessation of forms of suffering;
   - a lessening or cessation of resentment or ill-feeling;
   by the abused person, in relation to the experience of abuse or towards the abusing person. Notions of 'self-forgiveness' are sometimes considered in the context of relinquishment.

2. **pardoning**: this component refers to notions of absolution or pardon offered by the abused person, in relation to the abusive behaviour or the abusing person. Atonement or restitution may be regarded as necessary prerequisites but the consequence of pardoning generally means that no further acts of atonement by the abusing person are required.

3. **reconciliation**: this component refers to notions of re-connection, whereby the abused person is prepared to re-establish a relationship of significance with the abusing person.

Each of these components can have more or less salience within an individual's concept of forgiveness. However, no component is regarded as necessary or inevitable within the proposed matrix of meanings, despite the fact that specific components are frequently subject to judgements of essential importance and desirability.

Each of these components can be approached from a range of perspectives represented by the following extremes on a continuum of self-determination:

- **self-realisation**: this perspective is informed by a sense of self-discovery or spiritual awareness. It involves the experience of unsolicited or freely chosen decisions.

- **obligation**: this perspective is informed by a sense of expectation or mandatory requirement, imposed by requirements of others or fixed ideological positions.

When therapeutic intervention is first initiated, people who have been abused often appear to be overwhelmed by feelings of obligation, expectations and requirements by others to embrace various components of forgiveness. These 'obligations' may be associated with a pervasive sense of powerlessness, feelings of self-deprecation and a sense of limited possibilities about choices for the future.

This is not surprising given the political nature and context of abuse which constitutes:

- oppression and subjugation of individual's rights,

- violation of their bodies, achieved by deception or force,

- exploitation in a context of imbalances of power and privilege and betrayal of responsibility and trust,

- imposition of secrecy, whereby the abused person is coerced to silently carry a sense of responsibility and shame for the person who has abused.

In therapeutic counselling, the abused person may be invited to understand and challenge the politics which inform and maintain abusive behaviour and which promote such a sense of defeat and paralysis. The abused person is invited to consider new meanings, new attributions of responsibility and new possibilities for the future. This may constitute part of a 'journey of realisation' which entails a shift from obligation towards self-realisation.

Various positions, in a matrix of positions or meanings concerning forgiveness, are presented in Table 1.

Table 1 – A matrix of positions concerning forgiveness

	SELF-REALISATION	OBLIGATION
RELINQUISHMENT	**Realisations about possibilities enabling choice** Lessening of Suffering and Resentment – Possibilities: - to relinquish shame/responsibility for abuse - to lessen suffering/resentment but maintain outrage/sense of betrayal - to lessen suffering without relinquishing resentment - to 'move on' despite hurt & resentment	**Expectations and obligations** Requirements to: - cease feelings of suffering and resentment - pretend to feel no hurt or resentment - share responsibility for abuse in order to: - placate others - accommodate to other's needs - submit to religious/cultural ideologies - be ready to move on
PARDONING	**Choices about pardoning** Entitlements to: - relinquish suffering/resentment without pardoning - decline attempts at restitution - remain sceptical about attempts at restitution - be open to restitution without needing to pardon - freely decide whether or not to pardon either : - the abusing person - the abusive behaviour/betrayal - seek justice	**Expectations and obligations** Requirements to: - excuse abusive behaviour - be open to restitution attempts - accept uncritically attempts at restitution - reciprocate attempts at restitution/offer pardon in order to: - placate others - accommodate to other's needs - submit to religious/cultural ideologies - be ready to move on
RECONCILIATION	**Choices about re-connection** Entitlements to: - freely decide the extent of re-connection - relinquish or pardon without reconciliation - reconcile without pardoning - 'move on' without pardoning or reconciliation	**Expectations and obligations** Requirements to: - offer absolution - submit to practices of reconciliation/reclamation in order to: - placate others - accommodate to other's needs - submit to religious/cultural ideologies - be ready to move on

These positions are not regarded as either fixed or discrete. They remain fluid, flexible and changing over time. No position or aspect of a position can be regarded as either 'correct' or 'incorrect', superior to any other or as a necessary requirement. When we invite individuals who have been abused to examine the positions they may hold, along with the ideas that inform them and the political context in which these ideas were developed, there is generally a shift from a sense of obligation towards self-realisation. We support notions of choice which accompany this shift but do not presume any right to determine the nature of these choices.

These positions are occupied in a political context and are informed by practices of power, at the time of the abuse itself and in all subsequent relationships of significance. The political context influences an individual's sense of freedom to choose certain ideas and actions and the possibilities which are available at the time.

Young children, for example, will tend to have an extremely limited range of options and possibilities available, given their high levels of reliance upon family structures and family resources throughout the time of childhood. Young children must rely on significant adults in their lives to develop and maintain high levels of accountability to their experiences, feelings and needs, in order to have access to a broad range of possibilities.

To be prescriptive about 'correct' or preferred positions involves re-establishing an aspect of the political context and tactics of abuse; a context which requires the abused person to provide something for a therapist, rather than to discover their own understandings and meanings and choose and develop their own courses of action.

Accordingly, if we attempt to urge or encourage a person to relinquish suffering, this may only serve to discount their own experience of pain and promote a greater sense of limitation and helplessness.

Popular meanings of atonement

Persons who have abused may also relate to these components of forgiveness. Their ideas, expectations and actions are likely to have a significant influence on the positions occupied by others who have been abused. There is a significant interaction between meanings associated with forgiveness and meanings associated with atonement for abusive behaviour.

The concept of atonement is equally confused by a range of attributions of meaning, as is the concept of forgiveness. Popular notions of atonement generally relate to notions of *acknowledgement* of abusive behaviour, *restitution* to the abused person and *resolution* or moving on.

Positions regarding all three concepts may be occupied from a perspective of *self-centred thinking*, whereby the person who has abused is primarily pre-occupied with his[2] own theories and notions regarding the abused person's experience and his own concerns, fears and hopes about his future.

At the other end of a continuum of consideration, is the perspective of *other-centred thinking*, whereby the person who has abused is primarily concerned with and seeking to understand the experience and effects of abuse upon the abused person. This perspective is informed by an understanding of the political context of abuse and an appreciation of the need to be fully accountable to the experiences and needs of those who have been subjected to the abuse.

As the person who has abused develops his 'journey of atonement', which may involve acceptance of responsibility and restitution for his actions, he may begin to invest in processes and practices of:

- **realisation,** which when approached from an *other-centred* perspective leads to acknowledgement concerning the nature and inevitability of the abused person's feelings of hurt, betrayal and resentment. From this perspective, he is prepared to face (rather than avoid) feelings of shame and remorse concerning the impact of his abusive actions upon the abused person and others. This 'taking on the burden' of shame and responsibility may complement the experience of relinquishment of suffering by the abused person.

  Alternatively, he may maintain a *self-centred* pre-occupation with the desire for release from feelings of guilt and responsibility for his actions. In this context, he may expect or require the abused person to cease or lessen feelings of hurt, suffering or resentment. He may promote 'quick fix' solutions which do not require him developing a deeper understanding of the nature and effects of his abusive actions. Self-centred feelings of personal loss are confused with remorse. In this way, he may actively contribute to the context for obligation for the abused person.

- **restitution**, which when approached from an *other-centred* perspective, concerns an unconditional preparedness to take whatever steps may be necessary to make amends to the abused person or community for abusive actions. There is no expectation of receiving pardoning or requiring anything else in return. This kind of restitution is an act of extending oneself towards understanding the experiences of others, with 'no strings attached'. Restitution is a self-determined duty or responsibility which is based on a political understanding of abuse and its effects upon others.

  From a *self-centred* perspective, the person who has abused may expect the abused person to accept his apologies, to provide a pardon for him or to 'forgive and forget' the abusive behaviour. There may be a preoccupation with making an apology which is seen as a pathway to pardoning and absolution, rather than a self-determined duty or responsibility to the abused person and to the community.

- **resolution**, an *other-centred* resolution is informed by the knowledge that respect, trust and desire for reconnection may be irreparably destroyed by abuse. The desire for reconnection or reconciliation is not an expectation that the person who has abused has any right to entertain or hold. The capacity to 'move on' is informed by a sense of responsibility to make amends to the abused person and the community, by extending oneself without having to get something back and the knowledge that abusive behaviour cannot be undone or ever forgotten. This constitutes a form of ongoing restoration through acceptance of the realities of abuse and the letting go of unrealistic hopes.

  A *self-centred* perspective is informed by a primary focus on the need for absolution and the desire for reconciliation and reclamation of former relationships. The person who has abused may feel entitled to expect or require the abused person to grant absolution and resume a relationship of significance. Restitution attempts may be seen as having earned the entitlement to reclaim past relationships.

Various positions, in a matrix of positions/meanings concerning atonement, are presented in Table 2 (see pages 43-44).

We frequently draw attention to shifts in meanings associated with forgiveness and atonement as individuals and members of their communities develop understandings of the nature and politics of abuse and invest in 'journeys of realisation'.

Individuals who have been subjected to abuse and who at first experienced a sense of obligation to 'forgive', may discover a desire for relinquishment that can maintain a capacity for protest against abuse and a refusal to pardon abusive behaviour or to re-invest in an undesired relation-ship. Those who have abused may experience a shift in focus from preoccupations with apology, pardoning and reconciliation to acknowledgement, restitution and understanding the realities of the effects of abusive behaviour upon others.

Table 2 – A matrix of complementary goals in atonement

	OTHER-CENTRED	SELF-CENTRED
REALISATON	**Acknowledgement of the effects of abuse** A commitment to face responsibility by: - trying to fully understand and respect the abused person's feelings and experience - accepting culpability for the effects of abusive actions - facing and carrying feelings of shame and remorse which are informed by the effects of abuse upon others - having no expectations, requirements or demands for relinquishment by the abused person	**Desire for release from guilt and responsibility** Preoccupations with: - self-centred desires and hopes for the abused person to relinquish suffering and resentment - 'quick-fix' solutions which involve avoidance of responsibility - self-centred feelings of personal loss which are confused with remorse

Table 2 – A matrix of complementary goals in atonement (cont'd)

	OTHER-CENTRED	SELF-CENTRED
RESTITUTION	**Focus on restitution** A commitment to restitution for abusive actions by: - being prepared to acknowledge full responsibility - attempting to understand the full impact of the abuse - recognising that abusive behaviour is 'unforgivable' - making restitution unconditional – 'no strings attached' - having no expectations, requirements or demands for any form of acceptance or pardon regarding restitution Restitution – involves expressions of extending of oneself, through consideration of others' feelings and experiences	**Focus on apology and desire for pardoning** Preoccupations with: - apology as a means to achieving pardoning and absolution - reciprocity, whereby attempts at apology carry implicit or explicit expectations or demands for acceptance and pardoning by the abused person Apology – a means towards achieving self-centred goals of absolution and pardoning
RESOLUTION	**Focus on acceptance and restoration** A commitment towards acceptance and understanding that: - restitution is a self-determined duty that earns no entitlement to re-connection or reconciliation - abuse may permanently destroy trust and desire for re-connection - the abused person is entitled to determine the level of any re-connection An understanding that 'moving on' is achieved via restoration through extending oneself by considering others	**Focus on absolution and reconciliation** Preoccupations with reclamation and resumption of relationships linked with: - requirements for abused persons to 'forgive and forget' - premature desires to achieve 'happy families' - a sense of entitlement to resume relationships following restitution attempts/apologies An understanding that 'moving on' is achieved via obtaining absolution and the reclamation of relationships

Working with concepts of forgiveness with people who have been abused

When matters are serious - life shakingly serious - they can rarely be forgiven either directly or conclusively. Such events may take most of a lifetime to assimilate and most of a lifetime to forgive. (Dowrick 1997)

Forgiveness is not a necessary concern for all people who have been abused. Whilst most people want to relinquish suffering, interest in pardoning or reconciliation may receive little or no consideration, especially in relationships which lack special significance or a history of connection. However, people who were abused by a loved family member or carer commonly experience and may express, directly or indirectly, the desire to forgive. When assisted to understand this desire and the ideas and motivations which inform it, in a political context, a shift in the nature of the person's journey, from 'obligation' to 'self-realisation', is likely to be undertaken. This shift towards self-determination can enable :

- relinquishment to be considered as an issue quite separate from pardoning,

- motivations for specific aspects of pardoning to be delineated and clarified,

- issues of relinquishment and pardoning to be considered separately from reconciliation.

The desire for relinquishment – obligation to self-realisation

Interest in forgiveness can stem from a personal desire for relinquishment from suffering or from feelings of resentment. However, 'obligations' or 'requirements' often complicate movement towards self-determination. The desire for relinquishment and the 'need' to pardon often become intertwined and confused.

Some people experience a need to understand or make sense of the motivations of the abusing person, in order to pardon and then to be able to 'move on'. This 'need' can lead to paralysing preoccupations. People who have been abused may initially be highly preoccupied with a search for reasons as to why the loved one may have done such a thing: Were they sick?; Were they abused themselves as children?; Was the abuse caused by something over which that person had no control? Under these circumstances, the abused person may feel an obligatory prerequisite for relinquishment. 'Moving on' is thought to be possible only by being able to pardon after having discovered 'forgivable' motivations or reasons for the abusive behaviour. This preoccupation may be reinforced by the abusing person's or other family members' attempts to excuse or justify the abusive actions. Sadly, this desperate need to make meaning by searching for causality often contributes to the attribution of self-blame through the ubiquitous preoccupation, Why me? – Was it something about me that made him do it?; Did I deserve it?

A political understanding of abuse

When considerations about forgiveness are informed by a political understanding of abuse, responsibility can be clearly attributed to those who have perpetrated or supported the abusive actions. Understandings about the nature and abuse of power relations and privilege lead to realisations about the politics of deception, the taking of unfair advantage and the construction of realities in which the abused person is obliged to feel some culpability. The actions of the abusing person and significant others whose responses or presence were important at the time, may be viewed from a different perspective which in turn allows for a re-evaluation of the abused person's beliefs about culpability and self-worth. The relinquishment of feelings of responsibility and shame and a lessening of suffering become possibilities.

A political understanding can enable clarification of the desire for relinquishment in the context of the nature of forgiveness. It then becomes conceivable to lessen suffering by relinquishing a sense of responsibility and feelings of shame concerning the abuse, without having to let go of feelings of outrage and a sense of betrayal. It becomes possible to consider relinquishment without necessarily choosing to pardon. A political understanding of abuse enables the drawing of important distinctions between 'forgiving' and 'excusing', in relation to the abusing person and the experience of abusive behaviour.

Understanding the desire to pardon

The meanings attributed to 'forgiveness' are always determined by the context in which the person who has been abused lives and relates to others. In a context of obligation, the 'need' to pardon is often seen as a requirement for relinquishment of suffering and resentment and the ability to 'move on'. An examination of the political context of obligation and the nature of and motivations for pardoning, can enable independent consideration of both relinquishment and pardoning.

At the very beginning of Mary's first meeting at a sexual assault counselling service, she handed the counsellor a letter and asked her to read it before engaging in any conversation. It was a thoughtfully written letter to her uncle who had sexually abused Mary during childhood. The letter did not name abuse as such, but referred to 'events of the past' that were now forgiven by her. He was being offered a pardon. She enquired after his health and wished him well. She mentioned the importance of goodwill between family members. There was no suggestion at all of reconciliation. The letter was in an addressed envelope with a stamp, ready to be posted. However, she had made an appointment with a counsellor before sending it.

Understanding the desire to forgive

The counsellor was intrigued by Mary's decision. What thoughts and ideas had led her to bring this letter to a counsellor before posting it? Mary was initially unable to describe the reasons for her decisions but she began to explore the history leading up to the letter being written.

Identifying a history of obligation

In recent years, Mary had come to believe that, in order to heal, she must forgive; 'The only way for me to move on is to forgive him for what he did'. This belief was understandable in the context of the history which she related. Mary stated that she had managed to disclose the abuse by her uncle when she was ten years old. Her parents intervened and the abuse stopped, but no-one ever discussed it with her and until now she had received no counselling.

After more than thirty years of feeling pain and anger, she did find the courage to speak out to a few family members and friends about some of the ongoing effects of the abuse upon her life. Although supportive, the common responses she received were that; it happened long ago; her uncle was now an old man; she must find it in her heart to forgive. Books on the subject of forgiveness were recommended for her to read.

Mary described the power and influence of these references to forgiveness. It was as though they confirmed some truth she had suspected all along, that she should be able to forgive. She felt ashamed that she had held feelings of anger for so long, especially when others in the family seemed to have readily forgiven her uncle.

Mary did not want to impose her burden upon others, especially those she loved. She feared losing their respect and friendship as a result of her intense needs and feelings. However, she was also sick of the emotional stress it caused in her life and wanted to rid herself of its influence. It was from this position that the letter was written.

Honouring ethics and values

Under these circumstances, the desire to forgive is generally driven by compelling obligations and fears and also by strongly held values and personal qualities.

Accordingly, Mary was assisted to draw distinctions between the obligation to forgive and her own desire to forgive. The personal qualities and values that supported her own desire to forgive could then be rightfully honoured and respected and these qualities were readily elevated over the fears associated with obligation.

Self-realisation through clarification

Mary turned her attention back to the letter and was able to consider it from a different perspective. She was asked whether she thought it would be important to make clear just what it was that she was forgiving her uncle for. Mary sat for a while in silence, looking at the counsellor before stating, quite calmly, 'I can't forgive him for that, can I'.

This realisation was one of many which enabled Mary to reconsider her position on forgiveness and to begin a shift from 'obligation' towards 'self-realisation'. She realised that she could not pardon her uncle's abusive actions and began to feel some entitlement to feelings of outrage at his treatment of her. Mary gradually began to recognise possibilities whereby she could begin to relinquish some of her suffering and 'move on' without needing to pardon at her own expense. Her desire to forgive and its informing ethics could be honoured and respected without having these personal qualities further abused or taken advantage of.

The desire to forgive may be informed by ethics which concern the expression of valued personal qualities such as caring, concern, compassion and loyalty, along with the desire for mutually respectful relationships. It is vital that we help draw distinctions between such ethics and personal qualities and obligatory expectations and requirements by others. Valued personal qualities can easily be inadvertently dismissed, mis-labelled or pathologised in the context of challenging 'obligations'. When this happens, counselling attempts can be profoundly disrespectful and can re-create a context which is abusive in itself.

A political understanding of the nature of abuse enables the ability to discriminate between 'excusing' and 'pardoning'; the requirement felt as a '*must*' that is associated with obligation and the sense of *choice* which is associated with self-realisation.

The context of childhood

These are extremely difficult understandings and realisations for adults who were abused as children to consider. However, they are even more challenging for children at the time when the effects of abuse are first experienced. Children are generally in an extremely vulnerable position, when it comes to these considerations. Their abilities to understand the politics of abuse, to attribute responsibility accordingly and to make free choices concerning forgiveness will be influenced by their levels of cognitive and emotional development and by high levels of reliance upon adult family members for survival, nurturance and a sense of belonging. Children face similar demands concerning forgiveness to those they face regarding disclosure of abuse; they are confronted by the likely effects of their choices on the adults of significance in their lives.

Bruno was sexually abused, between the ages of 8 and 9 years, by an older male cousin. This abuse took place at extended family gatherings where the children were encouraged to play on their own whilst the adults enjoyed card games. Bruno was a boy lacking in confidence and he put up with the abuse for a long time before disclosing to his older sister. Bruno's parents also lacked confidence and status at family gatherings where they were treated as 'poor cousins' by other family members. Bruno was attuned to his parent's feelings and he put off disclosing the abuse 'so that Mum and Dad wouldn't be picked on'.

Following his disclosure, Bruno and his parents were accused of lying. When his cousin eventually made a partial admission, the abuse was minimised along with any effects it might have upon Bruno. Bruno was pressured by his grandparents to forgive his cousin, with assurances that it would never happen again. Bruno's parents also felt obliged to encourage him to forgive. He was expected to continue to attend family gatherings and to maintain an ongoing relationship with his cousin. In this context of obligation, forgiveness is a requirement, as the restoration and maintenance of family connectedness is pursued at the expense of Bruno's feelings and needs.

Considerations about forgiveness by children, following sexual abuse, are highly influenced by the attitudes and positions taken by significant adults in their lives. Children rely upon adults to make decisions and take action in (the children's) best interests. When adult caregivers are themselves struggling to balance others' expectations and obligations with their own feelings, their children's needs and feelings can be overlooked and sacrificed, for the sake of family harmony, to placate others, to avoid personal distress or to submit to religious or cultural beliefs. In this context, accommodation to adult caregivers' expectations and hopes may be the only effective choice for many children. As a result, they are likely to form enduring beliefs about culpability and the obligation to forgive which may persist long into adulthood and limit a sense of choice.

A life-long journey

'Journeys of realisation' tend to be life-long, beginning in childhood and continuing into adulthood. The balance between self-realisation and sense of obligation, at a particular time, sets a context for the nature of investment in a range of ideas about forgiveness.

Anna is currently 23 years old and has experienced a range of demands, hopes and confusions, in relation to aspects of forgiveness, over the past 13 years. Both Anna, and her older sister Tanya, were sexually abused by their father. He commenced this abuse when Anna was 8 years old and her sister was in early adolescence. He subsequently served a two year prison sentence for the abuse.

At ten years old – a context for obligation

When Anna was 10 years old and just prior to her father's release from prison, she was referred with her mother and sister for counselling. Sadly, they had received no counselling help prior to this time. The family was experiencing conflict regarding the father wanting to return to the family home. This was the mother's preference. She spoke of having little extended family support and felt incapable of coping with the demands of being a single parent. Anna's mother was also concerned about deterioration in her health and was quite despairing about coping in the future. Two younger male siblings were reported as missing their father terribly and wanting him home. Tanya, the older daughter, was raising strong opposition to her father returning home. The mother was feeling extremely hurt that Tanya seemed unable to understand or appreciate her position and needs.

Anna was highly sensitive and attuned to both her mother's and her sister's positions. She appeared to be quietly weighing up all family members' feelings and positions before tentatively expressing support for her mother's preference. Anna did express disgust about her father's abusive behaviour, naming it as 'dirty'. However, she was extremely concerned about her mother's and brothers' feelings of grief, in relation to the father's absence from the family. She was hopeful that the help her father had received in prison would mean he wouldn't do it again and she was prepared to accept as reassurance the promise that both daughters could have locks on their bedroom doors.

Anna's journey began in a context of obligation to forgive (relinquish, pardon and re-unite with) her father in order to support and protect her mother's and her brothers' needs.

At 14 years old – realisations and hopes for restitution

When Anna was 14 years old, she sought counselling on her own initiative. She had begun to think and feel differently about her father's past actions and current circumstances within the family, once her father returned home. She had decided to leave home when she was 12 years old. Anna was taking significant steps in a shift in thinking and action, from obligation towards self-realisation. She was now more able to consider and explore the personal and political nature and implications of her father's abusive behaviour. Anna began to experience an increased sense of outrage as she spoke of realisations that her father's abusive behaviour was sexually motivated; 'I thought it was a dirty thing he did but I wanted to forgive him, but now I know what he was thinking and feeling'. She began to identify ways that her father had tricked, manipulated and silenced her. Anna was now in a position to acknowledge and appreciate her own needs and feelings separate from those of family members. This allowed for honouring of her personal qualities including courage, determination, sensitivity and protectiveness towards others, as well as expressions of outrage and strong statements about her rights to safety and respect.

From this perspective of self-realisation, Anna took significant steps to relinquish a sense of responsibility for the abuse whilst maintaining strong feelings of outrage. She used this perspective to inform important life choices. However, alongside this, she also experienced strong feelings of grief and concern about her family. Ideally she wanted circumstances to change so that she could live at home. She wanted her mother to take a stronger role in the family, 'Why does she always go along with him as though he's the most important one in the family?' She wanted her father to show remorse and open himself to understanding the effects that his abusive behaviour had on her life, instead of, 'acting as though nothing ever happened'. In this context, Anna had hopes and was open to the possibility of pardoning and reconnection with her father.

At 23 years old – choices regarding forgiveness

Anna sought counselling again when she was 23 years old. At this time she was in a secure relationship with a child of her own. She now had no interest in reconnection with her father and did not want him in any way part of her life. Anna was now concerned with her relationship with her mother. She wanted a close relationship with her mother but felt extremely angry and frustrated and daunted by the intensity of her feelings about certain responses and behaviours by her mother which she experienced as contributing to experiences of abuse by her father. She felt unable to 'forgive' her mother but wanted to explore the possibility for reconnection.

Clarifying desires for forgiveness

Anna was assisted to name the behaviours and responses of her mother which concerned her and to have the stories associated with her experience listened to and honoured. She described numerous occasions when she had tried to disclose the abuse to her mother, but felt she had not been listened to or taken seriously. When her mother did eventually acknowledge her disclosure, she minimised it and seemed reluctant to involve outside help. Anna detailed how she and her sister had tried very hard to support their mother by doing chores and assisting with the care of their younger brothers, whilst her father was in prison. She recalled her extreme feelings of disappointment at her mother's decision to have her father return to the family home. Anna acknowledged the early context of obligation, whereby she had supported her mother in this because she was afraid of losing her and at the time it seemed selfish to deny her younger brothers their father.

Considerations for pardoning

At no stage was any attempt made to excuse or justify any of Anna's mother's behaviours or responses during this process. However, Anna was invited to name specific reactions, responses and actions that she might consider for forgiveness or pardoning. These included, her mother:

- *allowing her fear to stop her from listening,*
- *allowing her fear of coping alone to influence a decision that put the children at risk,*
- *lacking the confidence to believe in herself,*
- *making choices that put adults' needs before those of children.*

Possibilities for relinquishment, pardoning and reconnection

In naming these considerations, Anna was able to examine in detail her concerns about her mother and became aware of intense grief associated with them. Some relinquishment of anguish and suffering is possible when these considerations are explored from a grief perspective with ideas such as; 'If only my mum had the confidence to believe in herself' which might be extended to include, 'then she would most likely have decided not to have dad return when he did'. Anna was also able to examine the concept of pardoning in terms of deciding the grounds to determine which considerations might deserve pardoning and which may represent ideas or actions which should not be pardoned.

Anna did not hold unrealistic hopes that her mother would be interested in acknowledging or addressing these considerations. In this context, 'forgiveness' involved relinquishment of suffering and resentment along with specific pardoning of certain of her mother's actions and responses. Possibilities for reconnection needed to be examined in the context of Anna finding within herself the ability to accept her mother's inadequacies alongside the qualities she valued, and to adjust her expectations accordingly. Anna stated that she was committed to continue this journey because, 'She is the only mother I have and I want to forgive her'.

When the adults significant in a child's or young person's life act in ways which are accountable to the child's needs, feelings and experiences of the abuse, possibilities for relinquishment, pardoning and reconciliation can be enhanced and are more readily accessible and achievable. However, the accounts of abused people who present for counselling demonstrate that the desire to 'forgive' is seldom matched with an equal commitment to atonement and restitution.

The following example, however, highlights the relationship between aspects of forgiveness and atonement in a family where there is mutual commitment to address abusive behaviour and its effects.

Renata was sexually abused by her father, during adolescence. When she was 19 years old she returned home after a 3 year absence. On returning home she discovered that her mother had empowered herself with information and political understandings about abuse and her father had made a commitment to address his abusive behaviour in ongoing therapy. Renata was encouraged by the individual commitments and achievements of her parents and had invested, over a twelve month period, in re-establishing a relationship with them.

Renata was feeling positive about her decision, however, she had recently felt increasingly agitated and confused in relation to feelings concerning forgiveness towards her father. She felt that he deserved her forgiveness because of his commitment to address his abusive behaviour. She believed that her desire to forgive was genuine, yet 'secretly' she also experienced resentful feelings which she regarded as 'unforgiving'. This caused her discomfort and a sense of shame.

Renata was invited to examine, make meaning of and name aspects of what constitutes 'forgiveness' and why she might be pursuing these ideas.

Clarification of the desire for forgiveness

The counsellor enquired about factors that may have led to a decision to forgive. Renata quickly responded with a description of her father as someone who contributed positively to her life in many ways and who had demonstrated that he loved and cared for her, prior to the abuse. She also considered his expressions of remorse, evidence of his commitment to address his abusive behaviour and his attempts to atone for the hurt he had caused her, as further evidence of his love for her. She was able to respect her father for these things and felt love for him. She explained that she had been able to forgive him in many ways but now wanted to 'truly forgive'.

Considerations for pardoning

Renata was then assisted to name aspects of her father's behaviour and qualities that she had been able to forgive. She described having made painful realisations 'about weaknesses' in her father, when she was addressing the effects of the abuse on her life. As she came to terms with the disillusionment associated with the reality of these characteristics, she felt able to pardon him for them, particularly in light of her father's changes. These 'weaknesses' included:

- *falseness*
- *patheticness*
- *sneakiness*
- *self-centredness*
- *double standards*

Possibilities for pardoning and relinquishment

When asked to name what she has felt unable to forgive, Renata was able to draw a distinction between her father as a person and his abusive behaviour. She felt able to forgive her father for what she considered his weakness of character but considered there to be 'no excuse' for his abusive behaviour. The abusive behaviour she decided was inexcusable and therefore unforgivable or unable to be pardoned. After some time for reflection, Renata commented about a growing sense of entitlement, to take a strong position around abusive behaviour, that was replacing the sense of shame which had originally concerned her.

Specific enquiries about the nature, purpose and meanings of forgiveness, when interest in pardoning is a consideration, are frequently enabling for individuals who have been abused and who are worried or confused about direction in a 'journey of realisation'.

- What is this journey about; desires for relinquishment, pardoning or reconciliation?
- What or who is to be forgiven/pardoned; the person? the abusive behaviour? specific qualities about the person?

- What forms of restoration are required or desired?
- Has the abusing person demonstrated signs of remorse or responsibility?
- Are there remembered qualities about the abusing person that might be addressed separately from the abusive behaviour?
- What makes such a journey worth the effort?

A clarification of the nature of and motivations for specific aspects of forgiveness can enable specific self-determined investments in pardoning and reconnection to coexist with a strong position of outrage and protest regarding abusive behaviour. The clarification of issues of pardoning can then inform further relinquishment of feelings of shame and responsibility in relation to the effects of abuse.

Such considerations concerning pardoning involve intense and painful reflection about intricate details of relationships which have been and may still remain of major significance. A 'journey of realisation', which includes aspects of pardoning, requires intense self-examination in terms of beliefs, values and hopes about relationships of significance as well as questioning about the ethics and motivations of others. In this context, relinquishment and pardoning inevitably become incorporated into the experience of intense grief. Betrayal is characteristic of child sexual abuse. The sense of security and faith in the abusing person and in the relationship is shattered and new realities need to be established. This involves a sense of loss and a yearning for valued aspects of the relationship which were apparent prior to the abuse and for the lost potential of what the relationship could have been without the abuse.

There may be a desire for some form of restoration that does not necessarily involve pardoning or reconnection. A struggle is required to take new steps and make new meanings that will enable some form of positive connections, despite past experiences, as part of a new reality. This involves an arduous journey which requires determination and commitment to holding on to values concerning love and connection, in the face of having been let down and betrayed in the past.

A fluid understanding of forgiveness

Events taking place in a person's life often influence long-held beliefs and positions regarding 'forgiveness'. Age, experience and new circumstances lead to the discovery of new information and ideas which can promote revisiting a position about 'forgiveness'.

An incident or interaction can serve as a reminder of past betrayal and hurt or as a 'last straw' leading to self-realisation.

Eve sought counselling when she was 30 years old. Throughout her childhood her father had physically and emotionally abused both her mother and herself. She believed that she had long 'forgiven' her father for his abusive behaviour but was shocked at her reactions to a recent telephone call with him. He had been rude and dismissive towards her and as a consequence she felt terrified. Eve began to recall distressing memories of her father's abusive behaviour. She was both outraged at her father's treatment of her and surprised that this behaviour would still have such an effect upon her.

Eve was determined to address these issues and to change the relationship with her father. She wrote to him setting out her current views about forgiveness.

'When I was growing up, as a child and teenager, every time you hurt me physically or with words, I always forgave you, and my forgiveness and love was always unconditional. I have never discussed our past before with you, and don't feel any great desire to do so now. However I do want you to consider what it might have been like for me growing up with you and mum the way you were. I want you to consider the impact of our last conversation, when you say to me that you've been putting up with my shit all your life.'

She added:

'I have never set down any conditions on our relation-ship in the past but I know that if we're going to forge any sort of good relationship then old patterns have to end. I never want to be spoken to by anyone, particularly someone I love so much, like you spoke to me on the phone. I don't deserve it. I hung up on you in shock and fear with that familiar blind rage in your voice.'

Eve realised that she had previously, always been prepared to pardon her father, unconditionally, and even to re-connect with him, after incidents of his abusive behaviour. Eve had never felt entitled to expect her father to consider the fear and hurt he had caused her. As a child she was not in a position to expect or require anything from her father who had never demonstrated any understanding concerning the effects of his abusive actions towards her and her mother.

His recent abusive phone call brought back memories and feelings associated with his abuse which she believed she had long left behind her. Her reaction shocked her and led to several realisations:

- *a desire to relinquish feelings of fear and distress,*

- *a sense of entitlement to feel outraged at her father's present and past behaviour,*

- *that her father was never entitled to gratuitous pardoning,*

- *a desire to re-connect with him, with the expectation that he take steps to make restitution by considering and understanding what he had put her mother and herself through.*

Eve recognised that her father might not be prepared to make efforts towards restoration or restitution in their relationship but was determined to no longer tolerate or excuse his abusive behaviour.

When those who have abused make sincere efforts to understand and fully appreciate the hurt their abuse has caused, a sense of restoration or restitution may be experienced by the person who has been abused. This experience can assist aspects of relinquishment without requiring pardoning or reconciliation in return. It can result in a broader sense of restoration of faith in the potential goodness or capacity for redemption of other people.

Working with concepts of forgiveness and atonement with men who have sexually abused

When abuse is first disclosed and made public, counsellors are frequently confronted by the initial reactions and responses of men who have perpetrated the abuse. These reactions and responses often include a range of highly self-centred and desperate pre-occupations concerning forgiveness. At this time the man is likely to experience intense panic about likely criminal justice consequences, along with fears of loss of significant relationships and of reputation and self-respect. He may engage in an intense struggle to avoid pervasive and overwhelming feelings of shame. In this context, self-centred preoccupations with aspects of forgiveness and insensitive ideas about atonement, are likely to be evident.

The desire for a 'quick fix'; seeking release from feelings of guilt and responsibility and reassurance that no-one has been seriously harmed by a 'never-to-be-repeated' lapse of judgement, may accompany any acknowledgements of abusive behaviour.

Feelings of self-centred, personal loss tend to be confused with feelings of remorse concerning the suffering of others. At this time, preoccupations with forgiveness can appear to be primary objectives with men who seek counselling.

When the plea for understanding and forgiveness appears to be associated with a self-centred desire for release from guilt and responsibility, this places even more demands and responsibilities upon those suffering as a result of the abusive actions and serves as a further abuse of power and privilege.

Steven approached a counsellor following the disclosure of his sexual abuse of his grand-daughter. He professed high levels of concern for the wellbeing of his daughter, the mother of the child he had sexually abused. He was particularly concerned that, 'she could not forgive' him for sexually assaulting her daughter. He went on to explain his position that, 'Her anger is eating her up and destroying what we have as a family'; 'She must learn to put it all behind her and move on – for her own good'.

Steven clearly felt that his daughter was under some form of obligation to him to relinquish her outrage and resentment, to pardon his actions and to include him in her family, to safeguard the wellbeing of all family members.

Not surprisingly, Steven's ideas are likely to provoke outrage in the face of the apparent injustice in his expectations and demands of forgiveness from his daughter with no obvious expectations or demands for accountability upon himself. Counsellors may be tempted to experience feelings of contempt and a sense of intolerance, to the detriment of assisting him to examine the nature of his ideas more closely. If we regard Steven's attitudes and expressions only as further reflections of his controlling and abusive thinking, we can miss opportunities to assist him to discover and explore ideas about forgiveness and atonement which might be fair and enabling.

It is vital that we do not lose sight of possibilities and choices available for Steven to make other-centred realisations. If we take seriously and explore his stated concern for his daughter's wellbeing, we may discover ethics which relate to genuine caring and a desire to understand her experience. He can be assisted to look beyond his self-centred fears and feelings of desperation. This may provide a motivational link to assist him to consider questions like:

- *What would it mean if you sought forgiveness without really understanding the hurt you have caused?*

- *In whose interests would you be acting, if you sought to have your daughter forgive you, without you having this understanding?*

By challenging our own intolerance and the inevitable tendency to marginalise men like Steven, we may discover that there is more to him than abusive behaviour and insensitive demands. We may be able to assist him to discover and name ethics which enable interest in a broader understanding of the nature and effects of abuse and investment in a 'journey of atonement' which becomes increasingly other-centred.

Beyond apology – towards restitution

Men who have abused may initially be highly preoccupied with desperate desires to make apologies in order to gain instant pardoning and absolution. The co-operation of a counsellor may be sought to support or give credibility to these notions of apology. Such self-centred presentations involve minimisation of the nature and effects of abuse and various forms of excusing and justification.

I just want the opportunity to say I am sorry. It is just not like me to do what I did. She has to know that I'd never do it again.

Apologies are frequently offered in the absence of any real understanding of the experience and feelings of the abused person. However, the abusing person may regard such attempts as sufficient to justify a pardon. Such conditional apologies are often followed up with bewilderment and self-righteous demands, when pardoning is not forthcoming.

I have owned up to it. I am coming to counselling. I have said I am sorry. She should forgive me. What more is she expecting?

It is helpful to draw a distinction between the desire to make an apology – which tends to function as a means towards establishing self-centred goals of absolution and pardoning, and the desire to make unconditional restitution – which involves extending oneself through consideration of other's feelings and experiences as a result of being subjected to abuse. Restitution involves a self-determined duty towards restoration but one which requires nothing in return from those who have been affected by the abuse. When atonement is informed by the desire to make restitution, the journey is understood to be ongoing and life-long. Abusive behaviour can never be ignored or forgotten and efforts to understand the experience of others can never reach a point where they are complete or no longer necessary.

Self-centred apologies tend to invite others either to experience a sense of accommodation and obligation to pardon or alternatively, a sense of outrage, insult and offence. As counsellors, informed by a strong sense of social justice, we may feel compelled to confront and condemn the abusing person. However, accepting this invitation serves only to reproduce the politics of abuse and further marginalise the man who is likely, in the face of our attack, to cling more tightly to his self-centred views.

The desire to apologise may be informed by respectful ethical qualities as well as self-centred hopes and fears. A conversation which challenges abusive behaviour, however, can commence when we listen and look beyond the desire to apologise to seek forgiveness and enquire about ethics which may support making amends for a wrong or doing something to help the person who has been hurt.

What difference would it make if you took a really close look at what you did and how it may have affected (the abused person) before you tried to apologise?

Men who have abused and who have been initially preoccupied with the self-centred desire to apologise in order to achieve forgiveness and absolution, can gradually be assisted to discover a capacity for empathy and restitution. They can be invited to find and name an ethical basis which supports a desire to understand the nature and effects of abuse and to make amends without expecting any form of acceptance or pardon in return.

Todd was 19 years old and a tutor when he sexually assaulted two adolescents who were 15 years old. When he was 25 years old, he was charged by the police for his abusive behaviour and he began to attend counselling. He was fearful of justice consequences and he initially tried to challenge the younger people's accounts of the events and to minimise the effects of his abuse upon them.

Todd expected his partner, Jenny, to support him and 'forgive' his 'indiscretions', despite her own feelings of hurt and betrayal and her worries about the meaning and implications of her husband's behaviour for the future. She felt worried and trapped in a dilemma regarding her love for and sense of obligation to Todd and her loss of trust and respect for him.

Whilst initially appearing to take Jenny's love and support for granted, Todd was invited to look beyond his desire to hold onto the relationship with Jenny and he began to explore the nature and meanings of caring in this relationship. He began to find the courage to examine and understand the ongoing impact of his actions, first upon Jenny and later upon the two young men and their families. This involved a significant shift from seeking pardoning and absolution to facing abuses of power and privilege and the ongoing effects of abuse, both within and outside of his relationship with Jenny.

In making these realisations, Todd began to change his outlook and he made a number of decisions that, for Jenny, were more characteristic of the respectful person that she had fallen in love with. He decided that he was not entitled to ask for or expect forgiveness or absolution. He had already taken advantage of two young people and had also taken his partner, Jenny, for granted. He did not think it fair to ask or expect anything more of them.

In order to address his abusive behaviour and avoid imposing even more upon others, he decided to acknowledge fully his abusive actions and to plead guilty. This meant going against the advice of his lawyer who was encouraging him to plea bargain. He began to acknowledge some understanding of the levels of hurt and betrayal that his actions would have caused. He began to understand and appreciate as justified, the feelings of

humiliation and betrayal expressed in victim impact statements by the young
men he had abused.

The response of the young men and their parents to the stand that Todd
was taking surprised him. They did not want the court to incarcerate him but
instead to sentence him to a process whereby he would continue to take
responsibility for his abusive behaviour.

Todd's example illustrates the possibilities for shifts in a 'journey of
atonement' from self-centred preoccupations to other-centred perspectives which
can then have significant implications for others affected by the abuse.

Beyond reclamation – towards restoration

Self-centred atonement practices often request forgiveness in the form of
granting absolution and reconciliation with the person who has been abused. The
offering of acknowledgements and apologies is regarded as sufficient to justify
the entitlement to reclaim former relationships. The abused persons are expected
to 'forgive and forget' the abuse and accommodate to an expectation to resume as
'happy families'. This may be regarded as the appropriate way for all family
members to 'move on' from their experiences of hurt and suffering.

This attitude is reflected in the following excerpt from David's attempt to
apologise to family members by letter.

I am really sorry. I will never treat any of you like this again. I think we can
make it work if you'll just give me another chance. We can put this behind us
and have the family we have always dreamed of.

David's self-centred concept of resolution is clearly influenced by an
understanding that the ability to 'move on', following a superficial attempt at
atonement, is achieved through obtaining absolution from family members and
the entitlement to then reclaim former relationships. Such notions can place an
enormous sense of obligation upon family members to accept the man's
understanding of resolution and can further traumatise those who have already
suffered greatly from the abuse.

David's initial understanding can be contrasted with other-centred
concepts of resolution which are based on concepts of accountability which

requires understanding and acceptance of the experiences and feelings of family members. In this context, 'moving on' is achieved via concepts of restoration through a commitment to extend oneself by considering the experiences and needs of others. It is understood that restitution is a self-determined duty that does not earn any entitlement to pardoning, absolution or reconnection. The abusing person is committed to trying to understand the potential impact of his abusive behaviour and the likelihood that trust or a desire for reconnection may have been permanently destroyed. The abused person is in fact entitled to determine the level of reconnection sought to be undertaken.

Statements of realisation – towards other-centred perspectives

Men, like David, who have abused, can be invited to consider more deeply their ethical positions, the nature and politics of abusive behaviour and the experiences and feelings of those whom they have hurt, through examination and critique of draft statements of realisation.

For example, the following excerpts from Terry's statement of realisation, regarding his sexual abuse of his daughter, have been annotated to highlight aspects which might add to a context of obligation for family members. The statement of realisation was not written as an apology nor was it shown to Terry's daughter. It was part of an exercise to assist Terry to examine and critique aspects of his own thinking and ideas. In this exercise, as Terry's respectful intent to acknowledge and address the impact of his abusive behaviour is highlighted and honoured, he is also invited to discover and challenge potentially disrespectful ideas and expectations (see annotations below) which are likely to further traumatise or promote a sense of obligation.

I am so sorry and ashamed beyond words for doing this to you. I shamefully got sexual gratification from my own daughter which is terribly wrong and my fault completely. You mustn't ever blame yourself for what happened.
- locates his own fantasies of sexual gratification with the abused person,
- raises the suggestion that she might regard herself as responsible,
- gives advice as to what she should or shouldn't feel.

I think you did the right thing in telling and not keeping it secret any longer. It must have been hard for you but I hope you can let go of the burden because it is something that I must carry.

- raises the suggestion that carrying a burden might be an expected or 'normal' obligation,
- makes a request of her to relinquish feelings and experiences.

I have been thinking a lot about why I did what I did. I was also molested by a school teacher when I was a child and I think I have never learned to show love and caring in a proper way to anyone in our family. I have let all of us down and cannot forgive myself for this. I will carry sorrow and regret in my heart for the rest of my life.

- raises a justification or excuse for his abusive actions,
- creates a suggestion that the experience of being abused may lead to the perpetration of abusive actions,
- creates a context for the induction of guilt and pity.

I am truly sorry. I hope that we can eventually put this behind us and have a better relationship in the coming years.

- raises an expectation for forgiveness and reconciliation.

In a context of honouring Terry's respectful intent, he was able to challenge aspects of his thinking and ideas in unprecedented ways which led to him taking significant steps towards an other-centred concept of atonement.

The steps men take in this journey often continue to shock and surprise them as they discover and challenge the pervasive and ongoing influence of self-centred ideas.

Peter, a 16 year old young man, was committed to acknowledge his realisations about his abuse of his younger sister and prepared a statement of realisation.

He declared that he was not attempting to ask for her forgiveness nor did he expect it. Peter tried hard to avoid any statements or ideas that might suggest that he felt she should be obligated to feel or to respond with forgiveness. He attempted to acknowledge the wrong he had done, that he was fully responsible for the abuse and that he respected the steps she had taken to stop the abuse by telling their mother. Peter's sister decided she wanted to hear his statement.

However, Peter was astonished at his own reaction, when his sister responded by saying, 'You know I do not forgive you'. He was surprised at her remark and then surprised at his own realisation that at some level he had still expected her to say that she did forgive him. He reacted this way, despite all his preparatory thinking and under-standing that he had no right to expect anything from her.

He was able to reflect upon and acknowledge this discrepancy and to challenge the sense of entitlement that led to his expectation. This discovery enabled Peter to develop a deeper understanding of his sister's experience of the abuse and to appreciate more fully her entitlement to hear his realisations and new understandings but maintain outrage at his actions and refuse to pardon them. He understood more fully his responsibility to assist his sister by carrying the burden of responsibility for his abuse on his own shoulders.

The following excerpts are from a statement of realisation, which highlights other-centred realisations and attempts to make restitution, by Larry who sexually assaulted his 7 year old half-sister, when he was 15 years old. These excerpts are taken from a longer statement (shared with Larry's mother) which Larry prepared after some 12 months of therapeutic intervention, during which he was invited to examine his abusive actions and their potential impact.

Dear Mum,

I am writing to say that I'm heaps sorry for what I done to Susie, and what I did to you and David. I sexually abused Susie and I let all of you down in the worst way. Susie was only seven years old when I started on her and I was fourteen. She trusted me heaps and looked up to me like a father. All the things we went through with Barry and I used to look after her and protect her. She didn't have a Dad who loved her and I was her big brother and I just went and abused her.

She didn't know what I was doing because I tricked her into it. I told her it was a game. She was little and didn't know what was going on but I did know. I knew I could have got her to do anything I said. I conned her and told her it was OK and just part of the game, and don't worry, it will be fun.

I know you want to know why I did it. I thought I must have been sick in the head. I've been talking about it in counselling and I think I picked on Susie because she was easy to pick on and I was only thinking about what I could get and I didn't think about her feelings. I abused Susie lots of times. I used to think about it a lot. Sometimes I felt guilty but then I would just lie to myself and say it doesn't hurt her and it's not such a big deal. She was a little kid and didn't know much and I just picked on her because of that. I feel heaps angry at myself for doing it.

I feel heaps disgusted and so sorry for what I have done to you all. I've caused you hurt and I know this will last a long time and that you won't trust me for a long time. Saying sorry won't make it go away. You all have a right to hate me. In counselling I'm trying to understand what I have put you all through and try to change so that I think of other people's feelings. I will never treat you or anyone else like this again..

When critiquing these excerpts, we must be mindful of Larry's age and the enormity of the task, particularly given that he had not had such consideration shown to him in relation to abuse he was also subjected to in his own family. Larry is attempting to take an ethical position in restitution which is other-centred and which also makes clear that he stands for respect and not exploitation. In focussing on political realisations about the nature of abuse and causality along with the inadequacy of 'saying sorry', he is trying to accept the realities of his abusive actions without an excessively self-centred focus on absolution and reconciliation. Larry is attempting to privilege desires for restitution and restoration over hopes for absolution and reclamation.

The following excerpts also highlight an 'other-centred' focus, with respect to resolution in a 'journey of atonement'. These excerpts are taken from a statement of realisation by Felix, who had physically, emotionally and sexually abused his ex-partner, Sue, over many years. Felix is attempting to clarify the nature of his desire for atonement and a need for resolution. He did not reunite with Sue but did maintain a relationship with their children. The statement from which these two paragraphs are excerpted was written as a clarification exercise and not as a message for Sue, however, she did ask to see it at a later stage.

Felix is beginning to understand a need for him to extend himself through consideration of other's experience and acknowledgement of his realisations, in order to be able to 'move on' in life. This desire has spiritual and personal meanings for Felix and concerns restitution but is not based on an attempt to reclaim a relationship with Sue or to seek absolution from her. Felix is becoming increasingly focussed on restoration by studying the impact of his actions upon others, especially his children, in order to prevent further abuse and maintain mutual respect.

I know you've asked why I treated you this way, many times. I've thought of lots of reasons but I know they are only excuses and justifications. The truth is I have been very selfish. I've thought only of myself and what I want and never taken the trouble to think about your or the kid's feelings and what is important for you. I tried to control you for my own selfish reasons. I tried to make you take on my ways of doing things because I couldn't handle you being yourself and living your own life. I thought I could bully you into submission. I killed off your love and respect and trust of me in trying to control you.

I am not writing this as an apology because I realise that I have made too many false apologies in the past and saying sorry can mean nothing any more. It won't undo the past or change the terrible hurts I have done to you all. I know I must think more about what I have done and how it has affected you all because I only thought of myself in the past. I am determined never to abuse anyone ever again. There are no excuses for what I did to you. I am disgusted with myself but I don't intend to wallow in self-pity. I will make sure I understand as much as I can about the hurt I have caused you. I know the best thing I can do is to stay away from you and let you live your own life. I know I have got a lot of changing to do and I won't do it by harassing you. I can't undo what I have done but I can stop being so selfish and think of the people I have abused and betrayed for a change. I can make sure I never treat anyone like this again.

Conclusion

We are continuing to learn about forgiveness and atonement and the enormous levels of courage required to embark on a 'journey of realisation', from the broad range of people troubled by abuse who consult with us.

The matrix is a representation of a range of positions, regarding meanings associated with forgiveness and atonement, that our clients have shared with us. It can provide a means of mapping experiences and has been helpful in making sense of the challenges and dilemmas which confront those who have been subjected to abuse as well as those who have perpetrated abuse, along with members of their families and communities.

We have found the matrix a helpful guide for reflecting on and examining ways that our contributions may promote self-determination in the journeys of those who have been abused and 'other-centredness' for those who have abused.

However, no schema should be imposed upon people's experience and there are considerable risks in using concepts like the matrix to interpret and especially to judge the reactions and responses of others. The matrix is a guide to understanding and we regard it as a 'work-in-progress' which is modified and updated over time. We welcome feedback and critique from others.

Notes

This paper was first published in *The International Journal of Narrative Therapy & Community Work*, 2002 No.1. Republished here with permission.

1. Alan, Rob and Maxine can be contacted c/o Nada, 1 Mary St, Hindmarsh SA 5007, Australia, phone (61-8) 8340 2240, fax (61-8) 8346 6115, email: nada@senet.com.au

2. We refer to the person who has abused as a male person throughout this article because our experience and research demonstrates that males perpetrate the majority of sexual assaults.

3.

Embracing the old nurturing the new

by

Silent Too Long[1]

This paper was originally given as a keynote address at the International Narrative Therapy & Community Work Conference in Adelaide 2000. Its title, 'Embracing the old, nurturing the new', relates to the ways in which Silent Too Long works as a group. The knowledges and skills of previous members of the group continue to inform the work of Silent Too Long, while the perspectives of current members are charting new courses.

Good morning. We are members of Silent Too Long, a group for women survivors of childhood sexual abuse. Some of our group members could not make it here this morning but they are with us in spirit.

It has taken us courage to be where we are today. Most of us are community women with few formal qualifications. To identify ourselves as survivors of childhood sexual abuse is a bold step and one that none of us has taken lightly.

It takes courage to speak of our experiences because of the stigma that accompanies the labels of 'abuse survivor' or 'abuse victim', and yet we have so wanted to speak. We want to express the voice, knowledges and experiences of community women who have lived through and survived child sexual abuse. We have expert knowledge about child sexual abuse, about how it happens, about the ways in which abusers gain access to children, and about the conditions in our society that have enabled abuse to happen. We have this knowledge because we have lived through it. We are the experts on our own lives and we wish to share with you this expertise.

Silent Too Long began four years ago when various community women attended a therapeutic group run by Northern Metropolitan Health Service to address the effects of child sexual abuse on women survivors. At the completion of this eight-week group we decided that we wanted to continue meeting for a number of reasons: to dispel myths associated with child sexual abuse; to educate health professionals and the wider public; and to stand in solidarity with other women survivors. Several of the original members have now moved on, however, they continue this work in their everyday lives. Other women have more recently joined the group, and so the work of Silent Too Long continues. Today, Silent Too Long has a number of projects underway which include running an open group for other women survivors, producing pamphlets and information, and presenting at seminars and conferences.

In this presentation, we are going to read to you a number of quotes about our experiences of surviving child sexual abuse. The quotes are all from Silent Too Long members, but are not necessarily the words of the women who are speaking today.

Please note that we can only speak of the experiences of women survivors, as we have only worked with women.

Our presentation is arranged into the following sections:

- First steps towards healing.
- The restraints we have to overcome.
- What has helped us to overcome the hurdles.
- Playing a part in broader change.

First steps towards healing

The first steps on a healing journey can sometimes be the hardest.

The search

The first step was searching, searching, searching for someone who I could share my secret with and who would help me with the consequences, who wouldn't say I was mad or bad or that I deserved it.

Finding the right person

When I first sought help, after escaping the child sexual abuse, I was close to a nervous breakdown – shaky inside and crying all the time. The first person I saw was a psychiatrist. I didn't tell him about the child sexual abuse, but instead about a recent incident at my flat. My family chose to believe my stepfather's lies about what he did to me, and they turned against me. The incident at my flat involved my brother bailing me up outside the front door. He threatened to hit me. I was so weak at the knees that all I could do was tell him over and over that if he touched me I would call the police. While I told this story to the psychiatrist, he sat there with a bland expression. It was like talking to a brick wall with a face painted on it, as indifferent to my pain as my family. I didn't go back to him. Instead I found a counsellor who used a different approach. When I recounted the incident at the flat to her, she almost jumped off her chair with excitement and amazement at me, for the courage it took for me to stand my ground at that moment. Me – courageous? I only felt weak and terrified. She helped me to see the alternative story and it lifted some part within me. I had a long way to go, but that was the start of the healing journey.

Coming through the door

Coming through that door to my first support group meeting, and acknowledging that I had something in my life that I had to deal with, was the hardest thing I've ever done. I came with a friend. She answered the notice in the local paper. I said, 'Well I'm not ringing up, you can. If you go, I will.' And she did. She rang up and she just said, 'Yes, there are two of us to come'. We counted the steps from the shopping centre. We walked slowly because to go through that door was a big step in our lives. Doing it together made it possible. We had each other to lean on. Each week we'd say, 'Are we going back?' And each week we'd reply, 'Yes, yes, we're going back'.

Courage

It took courage to speak about the unspeakable. I thought that I'd never ever speak about it, that this was something that I would never be able to do. But as time went on that changed – now just try and stop me!

Wanting to survive

When I spoke up as a child about the abuse I was punished severely. To walk through the door knowing I was going to bring it up again was very scary. In talking about what you have experienced, there is always a risk you will be re-victimised. You don't know what people are going to say. But I was so tired of being a victim. I just wanted more. I wanted to move on. I was tired of being scared and tearful. Those feelings were stronger than the self-doubt and the fears and the pressures. The sense of wanting to survive and wanting to move on was stronger in the end. It got me that step through the door. It was good but the very first time was very hard. I was trying to think of every excuse I could so that I couldn't turn up that morning. But everything went really well. I didn't have a choice! [laughter]

Breaking the silence

I think the silence had already been broken because the group had been advertised in the paper. I'd been to many health workers before and had felt very silenced in their rooms. Coming through the door here was different because the silence was instantly broken. Everybody knew why

I was there. In some ways this made stepping in the door harder - it was like wearing a label. But in other ways it was a breaking of the silence already and that was appealing. When I walked into the room I was completely terrified, but then I saw that all the others looked as if they felt as scared as me and in a strange way this was very comforting.

The restraints we have to overcome

As survivors we face many restraints in reclaiming our lives from the effects of childhood sexual abuse.

We are not the problem

Often the first people we speak to in our adult lives about the abuse are health professionals. And often we are put straight onto medication or sent off to see a psychiatrist. We are pathologised, told that there's something wrong with us. Coming into this group is about being able to step away from that. It's about acknowledging the many parts of our lives that have nothing to do with the abuse.

Lack of family support

It is very hard to break contact with one's natural family and to live as an orphan. Emotionally I was always an orphan. Most people do not understand and cannot comprehend what it is like to live without family support. It is hard for my children not to know their grandparents, uncles, aunts and cousins. But my children's safety is my first priority.

Lack of justice

One of the things that makes it more difficult to address the effects of abuse is that often there is no sense that justice has been done, no sense of righting of the wrongs, no public acknowledgements that what happened was wrong and that it was not our fault.

Stigma and labelling

We've had to overcome stigma and labelling. We live in a culture which even today is still very quick to blame women for abuse. Coming through that door takes a lot of courage because it's saying, 'I'm not prepared to stand with the myths any more'. Self-doubt, shame, blame and anxiety are huge things that try to keep women isolated and silenced. We have to overcome a lot, and keep overcoming a lot, to speak out.

Not being believed

My greatest fear in coming to the group was, 'They probably won't believe me'.

Self-doubt

I think self-doubt is such a huge issue. We've talked a lot about it in the group. A fairly major effect of child sexual abuse is to doubt yourself, to doubt your own sanity, especially if other people around you have never given you credence for what's actually happened. The self-doubt can build and build and leave you thinking there's something wrong with yourself.

Blame

When I came here I just didn't want to hear any more that the child sexual abuse was my fault. I was so tired of hearing that. I kept thinking, 'I can't be that bad, I can't remember ever being that bad'.

Leaving the past in the past

It hurts a lot when people say to you, can't you leave the past in the past. Even well-intentioned loving friends can say it at times. That attitude, no matter how subtle, has often crushed me and made me feel so alien. It has made me think, 'What is wrong with me? Why can't I just let it go?' I tried to be happy for others and keep silent, but a deep wave of sadness kept washing over me. If I ever talked about how I felt, they would ask why I was hanging onto the past, or sigh, which felt the same. I had to live through the abuse every minute for fourteen years, but others didn't seem to be able to listen for one second. A heavy heart cannot heal in silence.

We can't just forget our past. That is asking us to forget who we are. How we survived and suffered is a part of our history, of who we are. If I deny the part of me that experienced pain then I am denying myself. Someone always turned their back on me throughout my childhood and ignored everything I went through. I cannot turn my back on myself. If I try to forget, then the incredible anguish that I went through can seem as if it did not exist in the eyes of others. This can make me feel crazy. It is as if I have joined with the people who tried to make it not important. I have to remember what happened and I need to speak about it, to increase awareness and work for those women and children who are still struggling with abuse. We have to face who we are, all that we have experienced and the ways in which we have survived. The stories of our survival are heroic stories of our time. They must not be forgotten. They need to be told.

For those people who believe we should leave the past in the past, I'd like to say that growing up with child sexual abuse is like growing up with fishing line and hooks entwined in your body. It becomes moulded and joined with growing organs, pain jabbing from unknown points, forcing you to avoid certain things so the unseen hooks don't pull. But sometimes, they still do, and it's not until you focus on an area, as if under a microscope with a counsellor, that you can see what part is you, and what part is fishing line and hook. Through narrative counselling you are able to gently ease that hook from that one part, and slowly, the new wound can heal. You can't leave the past in the past, because it is still inside of you. But bit by bit, through the healing process, hooks are removed and wounds can heal, but it takes time, patience and courage to undergo it all.

What has helped us to overcome the hurdles

In our experience of being a part of Silent Too Long there are many factors that enable us to reclaim our lives from the effects of abuse.

Understanding the difference between submission and consent – it was not our fault

My first big hurdle to overcome was to try to understand the difference between submission and consent. From the age of eight, I had been forced to agree to child sexual abuse because there were always dreadful consequences if

I did not. He even waited until the so-called 'age of consent' before forcing me to submit to rape. Growing up under the belief that I had agreed and therefore given up any rights, I didn't think anyone would help me, that they'd all blame me. I believed I suffered because I was weak, for agreeing and giving up my rights.

I thought if I was strong, I would be prepared to suffer the violence and even die. But I submitted and suffered alone. For this reason, I didn't escape the child sexual abuse for many years. Understanding that submitting to save yourself and others from further pain is not consent, has allowed me to release an enormous amount of self-blame and allowed me to see that protecting my own life and sanity was not a weakness.

Diversity

One of the things that has made a difference to me is that within the group there are women from lots of different backgrounds and ages. Seeing the older women in the group offers me hope that it's never too late. It's really encouraging. And seeing younger women there is just excellent. We all bring different things to offer. We learn from each other. Everyone comes out with these little gems that I can take away with me. They get me through until the next week.

Amongst our own

When I first sat down amongst the group I thought, 'Oh my god, more experts'. But when they each stood up and said, 'I'm a survivor of child sexual abuse', it was just incredible. It brought me back.

Belief

Walking into this group I knew that whoever was there would believe me. Sometimes, because there is so much pretence, disbelief and silence, I can doubt my own reality. I still have trouble believing it happened. I don't want it to be true, but it is. But sitting and listening to other women's stories, it is different. I can honestly say, 'I do understand you and I believe you. What you are saying is the truth.' It changes it for me too. I am believed.

Naming the effects of abuse

Once we give names to the effects of abuse that we are experiencing, we can find ways to pre-empt them, to prevent them sneaking up on us. We can have more power over our own lives.

Being able to talk

Sometimes when the memories surge it can feel like I'm going crazy. To be able to come to the group and to be able to talk about that, to see how it happens to other people, makes the fear of madness a little smaller. With other child sexual abuse survivors I feel understood, accepted, as if I belong. Even though the details may be different, the themes of our lives are similar. I know the others understand most of my dilemmas.

Claiming our expertise

Abusers often say that they know us and what is good for us. Health professionals too often seem to think they know what is best for us. Sometimes it can seem as if I am the last person to know what is best for me! But no-one knows me better than me! Our journeys are personal, they involve us finding our own answers to our own problems.

Honouring the stands that we took as children to protect ourselves and others

It's been important to me to acknowledge the stands that I took as a child to protect myself - like refusing to be left alone in the house with Uncle Bill or Grandad even if I was threatened with punishment for 'being rude' or 'not respecting my elders'. There were also ways I protected others when I was small. When I was a kid I didn't invite other kids to our house. I couldn't stand hearing and seeing what he did to them. Acknowledging the things we have done all our lives to protect ourselves and others can be significant and powerful for our own healing.

Honouring our acts of resistance

After my father would rape and beat me, I would wait until he left the room. Then I would stand up. I would never let him totally win. There was a part of my inner-being, my spirit, that would never agree with what was happening to me. I couldn't stand up while he was there - it would have been too dangerous. He would have beaten me again. But once it was safe, I stood up. There was a part of me he could never get to - my hope. I knew there were other ways of treating children, that this abuse was not justified - that it would never be. In retrospect there were powerful choices and actions I made as an abused child, even if they seemed small and ineffectual at the time. Speaking about these acts of resistance, sharing them together has made a real difference.

Honouring the ways in which we have protected others from abuse

It's been important to us to acknowledge the acts we have taken to protect others - especially our children. There have been many examples, including: interviewing kindergarten teachers about their understandings of child protection; educating our doctors about child sexual abuse; educating other women in our lives; and calling upon the editor of the local newspaper to ensure responsible reporting of child abuse cases.

Migrating identities

The metaphor of a migration of identity has been a beautiful tool in the group. Visualising the travels we are on has really worked for me. I really like the way that a metaphor of migration teaches you to flow - to acknowledge that there will be valleys that we will have to travel through, but then when we come up over the other side we have a different view of ourselves.

Learning new skills

When you live one way for a good many years and then you don't want to do that any more, you have to learn new skills. You have to learn all over again. I had to learn to say, 'No, I don't want to do that'. It wasn't easy. It's only a little word, but for some of us it's not easy to say. We're learning all the time.

Repelling blame

The group puts the blame back where the blame should be. We say that the perpetrator was completely in the wrong. We were just little girls. That's been one of the key things for me in moving on in my life. As the blame lifted it was like a weight leaving me. It was unreal. It was magic.

Commitment to justice

An amazing commitment to justice seems to vibrate through the group. It allows people to share in honesty.

Deciding to love

There's been so much hate in my life. I've been a very angry, very violent sort of person. Deciding that there'd been too much hate, deciding to love the little girl that was once me, has made the difference.

Courage and hope

The things that really stand out for me with the group are the courage and hope and how we have just really held onto a knowledge that things could be and should be different. Somehow we've held onto hope and a knowledge of what is truth and justice. That's really powerful.

Viewing it as a process

It's a continual healing journey. We have made some mistakes and we'll continue to. That's one of the ways we learn.

Laughter

This group is good because, although there's lots of sadness and stuff, I love it when we laugh. In fact we've been told a number of times to 'Keep it down'. That's pretty funny for a group called Silent Too Long! [laughter]

Balancing sorrow and strength

It has been very important for us to acknowledge the sorrow that we have lived with, its impact on our lives, and to balance this with the steps we have taken, the things we can celebrate, the stories of survival.

Acknowledging the adjustments

I think it's important to acknowledge that walking out of the door at the end of the group is also a big step. To talk as a group about these issues and then move back into our daily lives is a big adjustment. I still don't sleep the night before or after Silent Too Long meetings.

Acknowledging alternative parts of our lives

Honouring, supporting and encouraging the parts of our lives not damaged by the abuse encourages us to move beyond being wounded victims. Some support groups don't let you get well. That's why I really like exploring the alternative stories of our lives. Even when everything seems tainted by what happened, the alternative story makes me a hero, or at least an okay person.

Seeing all the alternative stories of courage in my life's past, and dispelling manipulative beliefs that were used to control me, has been very important.

I can now be proud of myself where before I hated myself. My partner has played a big part in encouraging me to revalue myself. I've learned to honour all sorts of aspects within me. Today, I have fewer friends, but those that I do have are deep and genuine. I prefer it this way.

Outrage

Outrage comes from the recognition that the abuse was not our fault. Reassessing my life from the position of knowing that it was not my fault, brought outrage - and feminism became very attractive! I felt years of anger, rage and outrage at what was done to me and to so many children.

There are so many actions of outrage. The group process is often a forum for outrage. We acknowledge the multiple ways in which women can step into outrage. One of them can be just getting out of bed. The outrage is such that a woman says to herself, 'I am not going to let abuse keep me in my bed. I am going to get up and step into life. A good life is the best revenge!'

Outrage comes in all shapes and forms. What can appear to be tiny things are really very significant. They speak of women having a commitment to life, to justice, to keeping themselves and their children safe. For us as women to come together and acknowledge these small steps of outrage can be very significant.

Sometimes outrage comes at the strangest of times

I lost my dog once and the whole street went looking. And I knew that if I had told any of those people in the street about my history there is a good chance that they would have been horrified and wanted to have nothing to do with me. They wouldn't know what to do and they would remove themselves from me. But because it was a lost dog everyone knew what to do. I really felt like saying, 'hey wait a minute. I'm lost too – how come you're not out looking for me?'

Meditation

I have found my healing in meditation. Throughout much of my life I have been unable to find words to express many of my experiences. But through meditation I feel I am led through the unutterable. I suffer from panic and anxiety and it was eating away at my soul. Being able to sit still and meditate was what I needed to do. It enables me to carry on with my every day. I can feel myself healing. It is almost intangible and a very gradual process but it has been wonderful for me.

Reconnecting with life and the senses

Now when I burn myself I feel pain. Once this wasn't true for me. I felt nothing. I guess it's a good thing to now feel pain! Actually sometimes it was quite handy not feeling it before! But truthfully I know it is a good thing. I also never saw colours. Well I did see some, but never the different shades. These days I am just amazed by the different shades of green I see in my garden. It is quite incredible.

It is amazing to realise how disconnected one can become. I had a complete dissociation from myself. I didn't know what I liked. If anyone asked me I didn't have a clue. Slowly, two steps forward, one step back, we become more and more connected with who we are and who we want to be.

A two-way process

I've been in a dual role because whilst I've been co-running the group I'm also a survivor. It's been an amazing part of the whole process to have a foot in both camps. The group has had a gigantic impact on me, in terms of my own understandings and healing. One day we were talking about how we didn't want the effects of abuse to continue – things like depression, panic attacks or feelings of self-doubt and worthlessness. We didn't want these ongoing effects in our own lives and we had made a commitment not to pass them onto our own children. Suddenly it hit me like a ton of bricks - crash! - that this also meant that I had to stop the abuse from going on inside of me. That this was part of my commitment against abuse. That I had to take a stand against the voice of self-doubt and depreciation that can roll around inside of me. That I had a responsibility to challenge that voice of abuse. This was both a wonderful and a terrifying realisation!

I was trying to co-run the group and meanwhile this amazing realisation was dawning inside my head and heart. I was able to share this realisation with the women and they gave me their support to take this next step in my own healing journey. Being able to not only co-run the group but also be a part of the group has really impacted upon me. But so has just listening to the women and their amazing stories of survival and courage and their insights. The group has so much been a two-way kind of process. I think that's profoundly beautiful.

Playing a part in broader change

Our conversations within the group do not just help ourselves. None of us are islands. We don't live in isolation. What we do between us ripples outwards. We are able to pass on some of the ideas that we've come up with to others in our lives. Our conversations touch other lives. They enable us to be supportive of others. We have learnt to notice the alternative stories in the lives of others. We have leant how to train our counsellors! Our conversations are like unseen threads, fine but very strong, linking people together. We are creating a network of different ways of thinking about child sexual abuse. It is spreading slowly outwards.

A partner's reflections

The following piece was written by the husband of one of the Silent Too Long women. He sent the group this piece of writing about the changes he had witnessed in his partner since she had joined with other women survivors.

We've been together now for several years and over that time I've seen her pain and fear and deep, deep hurt caused by the sexual abuse. I've felt hopeless, wanting to help but not knowing what to do. I've seen the sleepless nights, the depression, the sense of worthlessness. She's my partner, my love, my closest friend, the mother of our children, and yet there've been times when she was swallowed up by the grief and the injustice of it all. It's like at times she couldn't see these other parts of her life. I've been unable to reach that part of her that has been hurting so badly.

But she's changing since she's been coming to the group. It's like now there is a place where the outrage can be heard and she can be helping herself and other women too. The other women have been in similar places and they can really understand where she's coming from. I still see the pain in her, but I see more laughter and hope. She's liking herself more. It's like we are able to share the same picture of her. And it's like getting my partner back from the abuse.

Cultural change

One of the things that we've talked about in the group is how our culture needs to take a stand against abuse. Up until very recently men's culture has believed that it was men's utter right to use women and children as they pleased. In this context sometimes individual men may not even think about what they do. We say this, not to justify these men's actions, but to make it clear that this is an issue that isn't just happening in one household behind closed doors, but it is happening in millions of households right across this country and elsewhere. We are calling upon our culture to make a stand, to say 'no' to sexual abuse. To acknowledge that it happens, how it happens and that it's got to stop – now. That's the impetus behind presenting here today.

There have been many examples of the ways in which we have taken action. First we joined a group ourselves. Over time, some of us have joined with workers in co-facilitating groups for other women survivors. Being involved with helping other people's journeys has had a big impact on many of us.

The work also ripples out into the wider community as women take their knowledges and educate people around them about child sexual abuse, its effects, and how it is a cultural issue. Child sexual abuse happens because the patriarchal culture in which we live does not/has not recognised the rights of women and children. We wish to speak more broadly, to be 'silent no more'. We have given papers at conferences and been involved in videos that have been shown in workshops to educate professionals. Now we're educating others, our doctors, dentists, hair-dressers, the people who feature regularly in our lives. A lot of people just don't have the information they need in order to be helpful. There have been many ripples from the work of Silent Too Long.

We have been on the 'Reclaim the Night' march a few times. Women have made banners about the group. To be out there in the streets with a banner saying why we are there has been enormous - especially for some of the women because the perpetrators of the abuse they experienced are still here in Adelaide. The women could have been spotted as the march was broadcast on commercial television evening news where the banners of Silent Too Long were clearly shown. Still the women carried the banners.

Joining with supportive women and standing together against the injustice and misconceptions of child sexual abuse offers us a second wind. For years we've felt helpless to fight against these things alone, but now our desire to create changes has been reinforced. We want to make it easier for others who are this minute suffering the guilt and shame of child sexual abuse. We speak out today so that others may escape as soon as they can.

We'd like to end this section on a short poem that sums up the spirit of this presentation. It is about embracing the old, and nurturing the new:

Yesterday is history
Tomorrow is a mystery
And today is a gift
Which is why we call it the present.

We'd like now for Pam to speak about her own story ...

Pam's Story

I was number 17 in the orphanage. They took away my name, my toys, the necklace my father made for me. They took away everything that had been me. By five years of age, I was a nobody. And I stayed a nobody for years. In time, it became safer for me to be a nobody. I endured years and years of pain, hurt, physical and sexual abuse. I was beaten, abused, locked away: silenced. I lived in a world of darkness and fear.

The darkness tried to swallow me up totally. It tried to take over my whole life, my whole existence. It nearly succeeded. It kept me tightly bound up. I could see nothing in life apart from the darkness.

But there was a light deep inside of me. It was a light of love that had been lit by the kindness of one of the sisters in the orphanage, Sister McMillan. She was the only person who was kind to me when I was that frightened little girl. She treated me with gentleness and caring. I kept the light of Sister McMillan alive deep within me. No matter what happened to me, I kept that light of love alive. I knew that if it ever went out, I would have died. But - over all the years, over all the pain and abuse and fear – I never let the abuse get to that love. That was mine, it was my secret. I felt no-one could take that away from me. It kept me alive: it gave me the reason to go on living until I had my own children to love. And until I had Silent Too Long to share the light and loving with.

Because of the abuse, I was a very angry person. My whole life had been restricted by the abuse. I hated the world and what it had done to me and to the people and the animals whom I'd loved and cared for. It felt like I lived inside a dark and terrifying tunnel. But always in the deep centre, was the light. Even until the past year, when I slept, I was always curled up in a cocoon, too frightened to stretch out in my own bed for fear of something happening to me. It was like that for fifty years.

Then just a few years ago, I found a counsellor, Susan, who listened to me, who believed me, who had faith in me. I cannot tell you how important that was in my life: to be believed and to be treated with respect. She helped me see other things in my life, she listened to the story of Sister McMillan, and she helped me bring that inner light inside of me out into the wider world. Through her help, I began to see light, colours, birds. I felt like I was being reborn: I began moving out of the tunnel. It was scary, but it was also wonderful.

Susan introduced me to Silent Too Long and to the other women who had been sexually abused and treated badly as little children. I met other women who knew, who had been through similar things. They listened to me and believed me. They shared their outrage with me about what had happened. They said the abuse should never have happened. They laughed and cried with me. It made it so real to be believed by other survivors.

We shared our stories, shared our beliefs, trust, respect, acknowledged our pain and recognised our strengths. It was such an amazing thing to meet other women who'd been through similar circumstances, who'd lived, who were strong, and who were loving and kind. I learnt from them about different ways of crying: that there are tears of sorrow, tears of pain and anger, and there are tears of joy. All of this was new to me. All of this helped me to step out of the tunnel and into the light of a new world.

I feel like a bird that's been let out of a cage. I'm free. I'm light. I now can have connections with other people, other living things like the birds, the plants, flowers, animals, people. I have been able to see the world through really different eyes. I get up in the morning and say how lucky I am. I've got a second chance. I used to wake up and regret that I was alive.

Now I wake up and feel at peace. It's lovely. I feel things from the heart now. I used to be guided by my head, but now I'm guided by my heart: I'm living heart stuff now. I feel that I have a future, and that's something I've never felt before.

Other people see the changes in me. My daughters tell me about the changes they see. I recently told them that I loved them for the first time in their lives. They both wept, but they are both delighted.

I've learnt that it's never too late. It's never too late to leave the darkness. It's never too late to tell my children that I love them. I've got my grandchildren now to love and I really enjoy them.

I can see the future, whereas before I couldn't.

My journey has been one from the dark, the cold and the pain, out into the light, into the wide world of wonder. This is a different story from being just number 17. This is the story of hope, and I thank the counsellor and Silent Too Long for making it possible for me to change my story. Now mine is a story from the heart.

'Gentle sun in a darkened room'

a song by

Carol Coulter

(Dec 1999)

There have been people, animals, toys in all of our lives who were significant companions during our hard times. This song is dedicated to them. The words were written by Carol. It is about her grandmother.

Grandma, you never knew for sure
The truth of what faced me before
I know you tried to lift the curtain
But all of us were sunk in fear,
Paralysed and uncertain

You didn't talk much
But your eyes were clear
When they rested on mine
They reached my heart
How deeply you cared

Chorus:
You were so much to me
Through the terror in my life
When I was lost inside
Your presence was a calming tide

Your love entwined
Your soul and mine,
Unfailing and unattached
To expectation

And whenever you gave
A smile was enough
To gratify
Your loving heart

Chorus

Anxiety slipped away from me
Beneath that loving blanket
As a withered plant absorbs as food
The gentle sun in its darkened room

Chorus

Beyond your death
And for all this time
You're still a shining light
Through the darkness that was mine

Silent No More

After singing 'Gentle sun in a darkened room', we then asked everyone if they could share in a moment's silence – for all those who did not survive childhood sexual abuse, and for those who are this very minute suffering through it in silence.

This moment's silence was broken by us all joining together to sing the song 'Silent No More' which was inspired by a poem by Margie Thomas.

Generations bring down generations
Filled with broken dreams
So-called happy families
That are not what they seem

We've been silent too long
Breaking cycles upon cycles
That have gone on too long
Showing the ugly side
That was hidden and wrong

Facing all the fears
Learning a new way
Because it can't stay like this
It cannot stay this way

We've been silent too long

And now that we've found each other
There is one thing for sure
We won't be silent no more

Acknowledgements

Silent Too long members thank David Denborough and Dulwich Centre for their assistance and for making this paper and presentation possible. We also thank all the women survivors with whom we have had many, many conversations, and whose wisdoms, courage and reflections echo throughout this paper. We dedicate this paper to them and also to our children for whom we hope the world will be a safer and more respectful place.

Silent Too Long – how did we get our name?

We were sitting around the kitchen table one day in the health centre discussing the effects of child sexual abuse on women's lives and the ways in which our culture makes it difficult for survivors to be able to even speak about the abuse. One of the women said that we'd been silent too long. We jumped up and said, 'That's it! That's the name of the group: Silent Too Long'. We will be silent no more.

Information and poems

We ask that any material used from this article acknowledge Silent Too Long. The poems by Carol Coulter and Margie Thomas are copyright and are not to be reproduced without their permission.

Notes

This paper was originally published in the *Dulwich Centre Journal*, 2000 Nos.1&2. Republished here with permission.

1. Silent Too Long is an action-based group for women survivors of childhood sexual abuse. They can be contacted c/o Dulwich Centre Publications.

4.

The church, confession, forgiveness and male sexual abuse

from an interview with

Patrick O'Leary[1]

As a therapist and a researcher in the area of male sexual abuse, the question of forgiveness is a pertinent one, although I see this more clearly now, than I once did. In the past, due to my own experiences of growing up Catholic in a school in which those hearing young men's confessions were also subjecting them to violence and abuse, I was not always open to the possible significance of forgiveness in other men's lives. In therapy contexts I would have been more likely to explore other areas of the conversation rather than open space for discussion about the meaning of forgiveness to the particular person concerned. I would have more easily adopted a position of condemnation towards the perpetrator of abuse rather than see the possible relevance or helpfulness of forgiveness. I would have been more open to survivors expressing outrage than exploring notions of forgiveness.

In recent years, however, I have come to see that for some survivors of abuse, forgiveness can be one of the few options available to them to move their lives forward. This seems particularly true for those who feel they have no option but to live in close relationship with the perpetrator of the abuse, or those for whom their entire social networks and family will continue to be in relationship with the person who was responsible for the abuse they experienced. I have come to realise that some of the people consulting me do not have the same sort of options as I do to sit in condemnation of the perpetrator of the abuse they experienced. This has been a bit of a wake-up call to me, as I have come to see how limiting it can be for a counsellor to take an absolute stand in relation to forgiveness.

How the question of forgiveness enters therapeutic conversations

The question of forgiveness can enter therapeutic conversations in many different ways. The most obvious example is when men come to me with their presenting issue being about needing to forgive someone. In these situations they haven't come to me wanting to have conversations about the effects of abuse on their lives, but they have come because of their wish to rekindle a relationship or forgive a particular person about abuse they experienced in the past. Invariably, it is not that simple. Once we get talking the men generally describe a range of effects of the abuse and their desire to forgive can be placed in the broader context of wanting these effects to no longer have such an influence over their lives. Often it becomes clear that the immediate impetus for them to have sought counselling is because friends or family members have told them, 'You just have to get on with it. The only way to get on with it is if you resolve it. And the only way to resolve it is if you forgive them for what happened in the past.' All the complexities of experience that this person may be dealing with may have been squashed into a thin understanding – that what they need to do is forgive. So at these times forgiveness might be less of a self-honouring direction. Sometimes we can unpack the complexities of experience before we go on to consider the relevance of forgiveness for this person.

In other circumstances, a man I am seeing might just want to explore whether forgiveness is a possibility. They might test the waters by saying, 'What do other people do? Do other people forgive?' This is such a beautiful question. It represents a searching for a way to healing, and also for an ethical and spiritual response to the experience of abuse. The other questions that people who have been subject to abuse sometimes ask are, 'Can I forgive? Is it possible? Will I ever get to the point where I'll be able to forgive?'

A third way in which the issue of forgiveness comes into therapeutic conversations is when people have moved to a place where the effects of abuse are less dominating in their lives. They may have already reclaimed much of their life from the effects of abuse and they are beginning to think about whether orientating to forgiveness might be a good thing to do. The topic might come up in the process of a range of other steps that they are taking.

Relating to forgiveness

The men whom I have spoken with about their experiences of childhood sexual abuse have articulated a number of different sorts of relationships that they have with forgiveness. The following list is far from complete, and of course the same man may move between these different positions at different times:

- Feeling responsible for the abuse and needing to explore issues in relation to self-forgiveness.[2]

- Being completely outraged about the abuse and not seeing forgiveness of the perpetrator of the abuse as a relevant consideration.

- Feeling as if they need to at least engage with the possibility of forgiveness because of their ongoing relationship with the perpetrator and their family members' relationships with the perpetrator of the abuse.

- Being willing to forgive many aspects of the abuse they experienced, but not all aspects. There may have been one particular incident or aspect of the abuse that they consider to be unforgivable.

- Wanting to investigate forgiveness of the perpetrator of the abuse as a way of standing in a different place in relation to their experiences of abuse.

- Having reached a place that they refer to as a place of forgiveness.[3]

- Having reclaimed their lives from the effects of the abuse and not being interested in any form of relationship with the perpetrator of the abuse.[4]

Obviously people's real-life experiences are much more complex than can be conveyed in easy sentences. For some men with whom I meet, re-telling their stories of abuse can open up a whole range of complexities. They may speak about times they have shared with the particular person who was responsible for the abuse that stood in stark contrast with the experience of abuse. In fact they may have shared times which had been positive defining moments in their lives[5]. The experience of positive moments in the relationship with the perpetrator can be diverse. Sometimes the positive acts might be part of the tactics that enabled the perpetrator to gain trust and power that were central to the maintenance of the continuing abuse. While on other occasions, these positive moments may be seen as more separate from the abuse. In these circumstances, these positive experiences can be re-acknowledged and sometimes this process brings with it thoughts and reflections about forgiveness. The man may then initiate discussions about whether they wish to forgive, or not to forgive, or whether they wish not to have a position in relation to forgiveness.

A further complexity arises when men genuinely feel very sorry for the person who perpetrated the abuse. Sometimes this is accompanied by a sense of pity, and some deficit understanding of the perpetrator: 'How could they have done that to me?' 'What does that say about them as a person?' It seems that this can be a process of re-framing the relationship of power in some way. While for others, there may not be a sense of pity, just profound sadness. I recall a number of men who experienced abuse within the church. When they have gone to court and seen in the dock the perpetrator of the abuse, who was a priest at the time, the men have said to me, 'When I saw him, he is now an old man. I had an immense amount of sorrow for him that it had come to all this.' This sense of sorrow does not necessarily diminish their experience of outrage about what occurred to them, but this sadness may sit alongside the outrage, and it may or may not lead to discussions about forgiveness.

In contrast to these situations, I have had some very interesting conversations with men who are now in prison because they were responsible for murdering the person who perpetrated abuse against them. Conversations about forgiveness with these men are extremely complex. Most of these men profoundly regret taking another person's life and some are engaged in seeking forgiveness for their own actions. For others, the reason they regret their actions is primarily because their actions meant there was no chance for a different sort of resolution with the person who perpetrated the abuse. By killing the person who perpetrated abuse against them, they ended any possibility that they might ever witness some expression of regret from that person. They were in some ways responsible for ensuring that there would never be any chance of acknowledgement or some different sense of completion with the person involved or with the wider community. Furthermore, some men saw that in killing the perpetrator of abuse this ensured that their own lives would forever be defined by the abuse. These men have been very clear in their advice. They have said that in hindsight they would have liked to have explored some other way in which they could have engaged in some negotiation of the meaning of the past events with the perpetrator. They wish there could have been some sort of process which involved others which would have richly acknowledged what had occurred.

From my conversations with these men, I have come to think more about how processes that involve individuals and communities in considerations of forgiveness have the potential to create opportunities for powerful acts of acknowledgement. It seems to me that meaningful forgiveness may not only require the person responsible for the abuse to acknowledge their acts of violation, but may also require some acknowledgement from a wider audience that abuse did occur.

Forgiveness and ongoing relationships

Undergoing a process of seeking and granting forgiveness may change relationships but it doesn't wipe the slate clean, despite what I may have learned as a young Catholic. As a young boy, notions of forgiveness were inextricably linked with the Catholic process of reconciliation which consisted of confession followed by absolution[6]. As I mentioned above, the young men of my school were in a complex situation in that those to whom we were meant to be confessing our sins were at the same time perpetrating violence and abuse. I recall that rather than speaking truthfully about my experiences of those times in confession, I would instead make things up. I was not interested in telling this adult man of my concerns, complexities, and moral dilemmas. Although I may not have followed the process to the letter, I did learn the basics – that the idea of confession was that we were seeking God's forgiveness for our sins, and that once this forgiveness was granted (which it always would be if we went through the process of confession) then the slate would be wiped clean, and things would somehow 'go back to normal'.

I think this discourse of forgiveness influences our lives in ways that we are not always aware. The problem is, this process does not work in the real world. In actual relationships, after forgiveness is sought and granted, the relationship does not go back to how it once was. It is not a matter of wiping the slate clean. Sometimes the relationship may be transformed in positive ways through the process of forgiveness, but it never goes back to how it was prior to the wrong being committed.

In working with people around issues of abuse I think that this is an important thing to consider. Let's take a hypothetical situation in which a young man is willing to forgive his father in relation to the sexual abuse for which he was responsible. The father's hope is that after his son's forgiveness, the relationships in the family will return to how they had previously been before the abuse had occurred. But the hope of the young man might be very different. His expectation might be that after the act of forgiveness the relationships would be very different from what they had ever been! The young man might expect that the relationship between father and son would be acknowledged but not re-ignited. The young man might see the act of forgiveness as a chance for him to move away from a problem-saturated identity associated with the abuse. The act of forgiveness, for the son, might mean bringing to an end the sort of outrage that he feels is in some way continually connecting him into a relationship with his father which is poisonous to him. The young man might be very generous in his forgiveness but the forgiveness may not be about a re-ignition of the father-son relationship. It may instead be about moving things to a different place. The act of forgiveness might be more a personal experience for the young man than an action which was designed to restore the relationship. In a situation like this, when actual forgiveness is granted it might be very significant and freeing to the young man and yet quite devastating for the father. He may be granted forgiveness by his son, but the relationships of the family may not be restored.

The significant learning for me from such a scenario is that even where outrage, anger and pain are present, forgiveness for some survivors can represent a possibility for healing and transformation. Forgiveness may not necessarily be an act for those who have been responsible for the abuse, but an act of freedom for those who have been subjected to the abuse. Such situations also show me how forgiveness can take many forms and that people involved in the same situation may have very different understandings of what constitutes forgiveness and what it will mean if it takes place. I think these different understandings of forgiveness are worth exploring as they may have real consequences for the relationships after forgiveness is offered or not offered.

The need for ongoing acknowledgement

Another area where these considerations are important involves the issue of ongoing acknowledgement. Sometimes forgiveness is spoken about in ways that make it appear as if it is a magical process. In relation to abuse, some people seem to think that not only will the slate be wiped clean, but the effects of the abuse will also disappear if they are just able to forgive. These are compelling ideas but they do not often come to fruition.

One of the related hazards of these ideas is that they can contribute to situations in which, after a process of forgiveness takes place, there ceases to be any ongoing acknowledgement of the abuse. There are many powerful examples of this in different contexts of conflict and abuse.

In circumstances where the perpetrators of abuse have acknowledged the hurtfulness of their actions, have apologised and offered some form of restitution, and have taken actions to ensure that no further harm will take place, the person who was subject to the abuse may decide that they wish to offer their forgiveness for what has occurred in the past. This is often particularly true where there is inevitably going to be an ongoing relationship of some sort. Some years down the track the relationships may be going along okay, but where things often come unstuck is when the person who was subject to the abuse wants to talk about certain situations, certain things the person who perpetrated the abuse may do that remind them of the violence, or that make them feel uncomfortable. When the person who was subjected to the abuse tries to talk about these things, it is all too common for the person who perpetrated the violence in the past to say, 'Well that's old hat. Don't dredge up the past. You forgave me for that long ago.' Similar responses are sometimes made by significant others who have not been responsible for abuse, but have perceived that past acts of forgiveness mean that there is no need for ongoing acknowledgement of the past.

This, of course, can be profoundly undermining and minimising of both the history of abuse, and also the history of what it took to forgive, what it took for the person who was subject to abuse to continue with the relationship. I think the idea that forgiveness can 'wipe the slate clean', can be very limiting in terms of ongoing relationships. Where the person who perpetrated the abuse can contribute to ongoing acknowledgement, this can make a significant difference. In situations where the person forgiving is going to be in an ongoing relationship with the person they are forgiving, I think it's pretty crucial to forecast some of these issues and to explore in some detail what forgiveness might mean for all concerned. What it might mean in terms of how the past will be related to, and what it might mean for the future.

Sexual abuse, forgiveness and the Christian Church

I'd like to return to the complexities that are involved in issues of forgiveness in circumstances in which sexual abuse has been perpetrated within the church. I know that some of the men I have spoken with who have been subject to sexual abuse are very much involved in Christian ideas of faith. For them, indeed for many Christians more generally, forgiveness is understood to be a really important expression of their spiritual selves and practices of faith.

For men (and women for that matter) who were subjected to sexual abuse within the church, the contradictions of experience can be profound. Not only may they be expected to confess and seek forgiveness from God via the very person who is perpetrating abuse, but they may also face a crisis of faith in relation to the issue of forgiving the perpetrator. For Christians, not to forgive can represent a failure to fully practise their faith. This can bring a whole lot of complexities into therapeutic conversations.

Different men whom I have spoken to have found their way through these situations in a variety of ways. I know some men, who experienced sexual abuse as children by church leaders, who have taken a very anti-clergical stance and have been outspoken against Christianity and/or the particular church institution in which the abuse took place. And yet I know others who have remained within the church and have continued to practise a Christian faith, and to join in the ceremonies and ritual practices that are meaningful to them. Of course, even this is complex. Some stay within the church because of the powerful practices of silencing that accompany abuse.

Like many men who are subjected to child sexual abuse, those men who have continued their association with the church may have chosen, for a whole lot of reasons, to refrain from talking about their experiences of abuse for a considerable time. During the years that they have remained silent about the abuse, the church may have become almost like a family to them. They may experience the institution as a place of acceptance and affirmation as well as being the key forum through which they practise their faith. When these men do finally disclose, so much of their life history and identity may be associated with the institution of the church and Christian belief systems that they may have very limited options in relation to forgiveness. They may feel an imperative to forgive for many different reasons.

These complexities are multiplied still further when you consider that within the church some of those who have perpetrated abuse also experienced abuse when they were young men within the same institution. In no way do I wish to suggest that those who experience abuse are likely to perpetrate further abuse, but in situations where this does occur, it can further complicate questions of forgiveness. The very people who are preaching the significance of both confession and forgiveness, not only may be perpetrating abuse against those they are encouraging to confess and forgive, but they may also have experienced abuse from the people who trained them in the very rituals of the church. If these complexities were acknowledged at an institutional level, it would make it possible for there to be powerful collective responses.

Towards collective reconciliation

This brings to mind questions of collective forgiveness. How can an institution like the Catholic Church for example, try to take collective action to address what has occurred in its past? Once again, questions of theology seem relevant.

As I have already mentioned, reconciliation in the Catholic Church has historically been a matter between one person and the priest as a representative of the church and God. In recent years, less conservative elements within the Catholic Church have held 'reconciliation masses' in which people don't have to confess to an individual but instead confess to God directly in the presence of the church through prayer. In these situations the confession and absolution occur as part of a collective group. There are no individual conversations of confession in these circumstances. But recently, the Vatican has banned 'reconciliation masses' and other forms of collective reconciliation.

It would seem to me that turning away from exploring collective processes of reconciliation reduces the possibilities for the church to find collective ways of addressing abuse that has occurred in its history. I don't think the Catholic Church has truly acknowledged in a collective sense the abuse that has been perpetrated by those in the church's name. There has been partial acknowledgement of individuals, but there hasn't been a collective response. There have been some church leaders who have spoken out about abuses that the church has been responsible for, but quickly other leaders have spoken over the top of them by saying 'these *particular* men were responsible for the abuses'. I believe that some other churches, including the Uniting Church, have made some significant attempts to acknowledge as a collective that the church has been responsible for the abuse of others, as have some individual Anglican parishes. If we are to meaningfully address the experience of people who have been sexually abused by church leaders, I think that some sort of collective process will be necessary.

If there is one area that the churches may be able to learn from, it is the ways in which Australia as a nation is trying to come to terms with the Stolen Generations. Various churches have been grappling with how to meaningfully apologise and contribute to redress in relation to their participation in the Stolen Generations of Indigenous Children. As a nation we have a long way to go but actions such as National Sorry Day, the Sorry Books, and the marches for reconciliation have seemed to be significant contributions in what is an ongoing movement of reconciliation between Indigenous and non-Indigenous Australia. I have no doubt that as we as white Australians continue to try to come to terms with the actions of our ancestors, as we think through issues of collective responsibility, apology and reconciliation, then this will influence all aspects of our lives, including our work as therapists. Engaging with questions of how to respond to broader abuses, such as the abuses committed against Indigenous Australia, will surely influence how we seek to address issues within families and institutions such as sexual abuse.

Acknowledgements

While the ideas expressed in this paper have derived from working with young and older men who have experienced sexual abuse, I hope that these ideas are of some relevance to work with women and children who have been subjected to abuse and violence. I particularly hope this because it has been due to the courageous work of the women's movement in bringing issues of violence into the public consciousness that work with male survivors of violence and abuse has been made possible. The development of my understanding of the complexities explored in this paper come from many dozens of conversations I have had with men who have experienced childhood sexual abuse, as well as conversations shared with a range of colleagues over the years. I would like to acknowledge a number of people who have been important in the preparation of this particular paper. David Denborough's sensitivity and skills in writing have been very helpful in shaping this paper while other friends and colleagues have played important parts in assisting me to gain clarity in this tricky area. I would particularly like to thank Tony Fletcher, Maggie Carey, Sharon Gollan and Sharyn Johns.

Notes

This paper was originally published in the *International Journal of Narrative Therapy & Community Work*, 2002 No.1. Republished here with permission.

1. The interview from which this paper was created was conducted by staff writer, David Denborough. Patrick O'Leary is a Lecturer in the Research and Education Unit on Gendered Violence, School of Social Work and Social Policy, University of South Australia, and can be contacted c/o Dulwich Centre Publications.

2. Self-forgiveness can be one aspect of a man's resistance to self-blame and can also constitute a movement away from self-deprecating ways of being and towards ways that are more allied to self-care. Therapeutic conversations in relation to self-forgiveness require caution, however, so as to ensure that notions of self-forgiveness do not dilute the perpetrator's responsibility for the abuse.

3. It is important to note that individuals' understanding of forgiveness can vary significantly. Forgiveness may or may not translate into an ongoing relationship with others associated with the abuse.

4. The decision whether or not to have any ongoing relationship with the perpetrator may or may not relate to the question of forgiveness. Deciding not to have ongoing contact may be a part of a process of forgiveness that does not include reconciliation or re-connection.

5. These positive defining moments do not diminish or minimise the often profound effects of sexual abuse, they inextricably contribute to the complexity of the issue.

6. The discourse of confession and absolution affects those who have experienced child sexual abuse in many ways. When someone decides to disclose the abuse they have experienced, they are vulnerable to many types of scrutiny. Some forms of scrutiny construct the act of speaking out as a 'confession'. In subtle ways, people who have experienced abuse may be seen as having to 'own up', 'face up' or 'show themselves for real' – in other words, confess (see O'Leary 1998).

Reference

O'Leary, P. 1998: 'Liberation and self-blame: Working with men who have experienced childhood sexual abuse.' *Dulwich Centre Journal*, No.4. Reprinted 1999 in Dulwich Centre Publications (ed), *Extending Narrative Therapy: A collection of practice-based papers*. Adelaide: Dulwich Centre Publications.

5.

From files of depression to stories of hope

Working with older women who survived childhood sexual abuse

by

Coral Trowbridge[1]

In writing about my work with older women who survived sexual abuse as children, my intention is to contribute to breaking the long silence that many of these women have experienced. The women who have engaged in conversations with me are all over the age of sixty and many have been eighty and ninety years of age. These older women have spoken about the effects of the silence that has surrounded their experience of sexual abuse. For many of them, the effects of this prolonged silence have become more severe as they have become older and more frail and when their lives are no longer busy.

When I started asking questions about the silencing of their experience of abuse I soon learnt there was very little literature written about the experience of older women. The first articles about childhood sexual abuse began to appear in professional literature in the 1980s – long after the women I am meeting with were children. I have also found that there are very few workers who acknowledge the experiences of older women who were sexually abused as children.

Throughout these women's lives many have consistently sought help in relation to the effects of the abuse and the lack of acknowledgement of their experience. And yet, these attempts at finding help have often led to these women receiving psychiatric labels and treatments (including medication and shock treatments) that have inadvertently contributed to a sense of shame, secrecy and self blame. In speaking with these women I have commonly heard self-descriptions like 'I am no good' and how various themes like loss, dependence on others, feelings of numbness, and difficulties in relationships have become the dominant descriptions of these older women's lives. I have also heard these women tell stories of attempted suicide, and their turning to alcohol and other substances.

Recently I have begun to think more about how these women developed ways of coping with the effects of abuse, and the lack of acknowledgement of these effects, throughout their lives and what the process of ageing has meant in relation to these survival skills. What are the implications of growing older for those who survived childhood trauma? What happens when these women become older and can't live their lives in the ways in which they used to? What happens when their bodies become physically frail and they need to depend upon others in their daily lives? These questions have made me think about the many older women whom I have met who are living out their lives in boarding houses – where their individuality has been stripped from them. What effects would these contexts have on those who survived childhood trauma? I can imagine that living dependent on the physical acts of others could contribute greatly to losing touch with their own ways of coping with the effects of prior abuse.

Thinking these things through has also led me to consider the many times when I have been introduced to a person in my work through a multiple problem-saturated description e.g. 'this is an extremely depressed women' or 'she has a long history of mental illness and depression' or 'She has challenging behaviours'.

In questioning these labels and in searching for new useful ways of working, I have found myself wondering about hope. Stories of hope speak louder than despair. I have become interested in what keeps hope alive for the people I meet with in my work.

Stories of hope!

I remember one particular older woman whom I met at my workplace. At this time I had been asked to work with frail older people who were extremely isolated. One of the first people I was invited to work with was this eighty-nine-year-old woman with a very thick file of twenty years. I shall call her Julie. As I began to read Julie's file I quickly discovered that she had experienced multiple assessments by a number of workers over the twenty-year period. Each worker had written, 'this is a very depressed person'. When I met Julie she was living in a housing facility for older people and she told me her eyesight was failing. I found no evidence of why the workers had labelled her depressed and, when I asked her about depression, she was astonished that such labels had been given to her. In asking about Julie's life she told me stories of abuse. She described being subjected to abuse from her father and then, after being widowed at a young age, of being abused by her second husband and of having to leave her family home. Julie spoke of how she needed to turn to the agency for assistance to find a home. She spoke of not having a voice in the decisions for her life. She spoke of abandonment by services and society.

Throughout the conversations we shared it became clear that the one thing that Julie had maintained control of was how she presented herself. Julie took pride in her appearance and presented as a glamorous and gracious woman.

When I asked her questions that inquired about her present hopes for her life, she said, 'to be able to put my eyebrows on straight'. When I asked questions about what it meant to have her eyebrow's straight, she went on to tell me that the thing that she had always felt in control of was her personal appearance and how she presented herself. It was a source of sadness that her failing eyesight was preventing her from maintaining this. We then went out and brought a magnifying mirror together.

Following this, I began to ask questions that inquired about other hopes and dreams that Julie had for her life and she told me that she had never celebrated a birthday. Julie said she was about to turn ninety and would like to celebrate this with her only son and family who lived interstate. We drew up a plan for her birthday celebration, whom to invite, where it would be held, and what she would wear. Julie planned a wonderful birthday celebration with her son and his family at a winery near her home.

Far from experiencing Julie as depressed, Julie was a woman who taught me about the need for us as workers to be acknowledging of experiences of abuse. It has been her influence that has led me to be open to talking with other older women about abuse and the ways in which they have managed the effects of this abuse in their lives.

Seeking alternative meanings of experiences of abuse

... one of the primary tasks of narrative work is to assist these people to
derive alternative meanings of their experiences of abuse. (White 1995,
pp.83-84)

This statement has shaped my work with older women who were subjected to childhood sexual abuse. I have become interested in trying to play some part in assisting people to break from the negative personal stories which have such profound effects on shaping the expression of their experience.

As Michael White describes: *... if we can help them to step into some other more positive account of who they might be as a person, then it will become possible for them to actively engage in reinterpretation of the abuse that they were subject to* (1995 p.84).

These ideas have influenced my work with older women around the issue of abuse. Here I will share stories from my work with Marge and with Jane.

Working with Marge

I had been meeting with Marge for a few sessions when she described herself as a 'nothing'. She said to me, 'once I was a beautiful child and my parents loved me very much, but something happened to me.' She spoke of how she 'got on with life', her earlier life achievements, and of how she had always tried to please people. She mentioned her achievements at school and how she entered the teaching profession at a very young age. Marge showed me certificates she had gained in her career and letters of reference she had kept. She tucked these away and said 'they are not important. No-one cares'. Marge also said to me, 'I have not told any one about what happened to me when I was a child and it's not really important now. It's nothing. Who really cares anyway?'

When I started to ask Marge about 'nothing', she told me first of her experiences of 'help'. Marge told me when she retired from work she 'suffered' a breakdown: 'It was my nerves I was told'. Marge went on to describe that once her 'busy life' ended she started having thoughts about her childhood. She asked me several times if I thought that she was 'mad' and went on to tell me about the psychiatric labels she had been given and of the shock treatments she experienced.

Phrases that may cause distress and have different meaning

Recently Marge rang me most upset and explained that a well-intentioned neighbour had suggested she ring him to get help around the home if she needed it. Marge had said she did not want to trouble him and he had replied 'if you don't do it I will put you over my knee and spank you'. This incident had me thinking of the many discourses of being an older woman in today's society. It also had me thinking about ignorance around language and abuse and the impact the above statement could have had on Marge now and throughout her life. I thought of the invitations in our culture to speak to older people as if they have no feelings, or as if they are child-like. I also thought about how this statement of the neighbour gave support to the dominant problem-saturated story of Marge's life, as it would to others who were sexually abused as children. Marge decided that she'd like to have a conversation with me about all of this.

A conversation with Marge

Coral: Marge would you like to start by telling me why the conversation you shared with your neighbour did not fit for you?

Marge: Well, I guess it made me feel like a child, yes I felt powerless. I also felt stupid and a bit scared. That's why I rang you. I don't want him to get into trouble. He was trying to do good you know.

Coral: Marge can you tell me what sort of values you hold in your life that this way of talking did not fit with?

Marge: Yes I can, I grew up respecting older people and was taught not to speak to older people like that.

Coral: I am wondering if you could name this way of speaking? What you may call it?

Marge: Yes, I think I can ... I would like to call it just 'disrespect'.

Coral: I am wondering Marge, if you can talk a little about respect, what it is about respect that is meaningful for you in your life?

Marge: Respect ... I wish more people had it, you know. I always treat people with respect but not to many people treat me the same. I suppose you think I am whinging ... look dear, don't worry, it's not important ...

Coral: Marge, your story about respect is of real interest to me. I am curious to know what I would see you doing in your work and in your relationships that is due to your belief in the importance of respect ...

Marge: I would never speak to someone else like that, I always address people Mr or Mrs for a start.

Coral: Marge, why is it important to you in speaking to people in such ways?

Marge: I have always wanted people to respect me. I guess you know I had no respect from other people when I was young. I always hoped that one day I would gain respect, and I guess I did in my work. Have I ever shown you the letters I got from people I worked with? But they're not important now are they?

Coral: Marge, these letters and certificates you received, who else knows about these letters of respect?

Marge: Oh the girls I worked with I guess … they know. You would not believe it, actually, just today one of them rang me up and invited me to a school reunion. I not going though.

Coral: Really? That sounds interesting. Should we talk about the reunion or continue the conversation about respect?

Marge: Oh the respect, sorry I side-tracked there …

Coral: I am wondering what sort of person has such respect for others …

Marge: Some who cares about others, I think.

Coral: If I were to ask the girls you worked with, what they would say about your respect for others? What do you think they would say?

Marge: Well they tell me I was the best boss they ever had, that's why they want me to go to the reunion. They say, 'it won't be the same without you there'. They always say you were so good to us, you taught us so much.

Coral: Can you imagine anyone who could benefit from your values in your work now?

Marge: Well yes I can. The girls at the reunion certainly and perhaps I could volunteer at the local community centre. You know, they asked me and I refused. I did not think I would be useful now. But after having this talk with you I can see other people might be in my shoes and might like a little bit of respect.

Shortly after this conversation, Marge went to the reunion at her old workplace and took on a volunteer role at the community centre. When I most recently spoke with her, Marge told me that she was keeping the voices of depression away by going to the exercise classes at the local gym and taking long walks in a park near her home each day. She is continuing to reclaim her principles and values with her volunteer role.

Jane's story

Since Jane has moved into a residential facility in which all her neighbours are older people, she has been controlled by feelings of 'anxiety'. Jane's daughter invited me to work with her mother about this anxiety which Jane describes 'the annoyance', which has become 'so crippling, so strong'.

Jane's daughter and a care worker attended my first meeting with Jane. They explained to Jane that they had contacted me because they were at a loss as to what to do about the anxiety attacks. They also explained that they had taken Jane to many doctors and that the prescribed medication 'was not working'. When I asked Jane who she wanted to attend the sessions and how often she wished to meet with me, Jane suggested that she meet with me weekly on her own. Jane and I also had a conversation about file writing. We agreed that I would only write in the files to document the days on which Jane and I met, and that Jane and I would both sign these entries.

When Jane and I met up on our own, Jane spoke of being sexually abused as a child and of how she had managed to live her life with this silence until ill health and the loss of her husband forced her to move to a residential facility for older people. Since living in the residential facility she has lost control of her life and anxiety has been present. When I invited Jane to give descriptions of her previous survivor strategies, she spoke of her love of other people and of animals and gardens. She said, 'Animals and gardens do not criticise. They don't let you down. You can nurture and love them.'

Over the time that we met together, I wrote the following therapeutic letters to Jane.

First letter

Dear Jane

It was great to meet with you this morning and to hear some of the stories you told about eighty-nine years of your life. I wanted to write you this letter because there were so many experiences you mentioned today that caught my attention and sparked my thinking.

I noticed that you mentioned the places that hold special memories to you. I also noticed that when you were telling me about these places you were describing their smells and aromas – like the cooking smells that came from your mother's kitchen. You also mentioned that you had spent a lot of time walking on the beach near your home and that you enjoyed the sound of the sea and the fresh breezes blowing on your face. The way you described how you have learnt throughout your life really struck me also. I am wondering how old you were when you realised that you learnt by listening to people. I have also been wondering who else may know that you have learnt this way throughout your life.

You talked about being a loving mother and a 'great housekeeper' and of how you taught your friend Mary to care and love. This had me thinking about this rare quality of teaching others to care and love. I would be interested to know when you first noticed you also had this quality?

When we first met, you told me about 'the anxiety' which you are now naming 'the annoyance' and of how 'the annoyance' was gradually taking control of your life. You told me how this annoyance thing stops you from going out and stops you from sleeping. You mentioned that 'the annoyance' has you believing you are no good and a burden on everyone one. I have been thinking about how bossy and controlling this annoyance thing was getting.

Today I became very excited when you told me that when you think about the nice smells and feelings, then the bossy annoyance thing is not around. You also spoke about wanting freedom from 'the annoyance'. You mentioned that you are noticing increased freedom from 'the annoyance' when you are out in the garden of the nursing home and when you are in conversation with your friends who visit you.

After today's conversation, I was wondering have you ever thought of writing about some of the memories you told me about? I was wondering how you might be able to continue to use these memories in your battle to be 'in charge' of 'the annoyance'. I have been wondering what might happen to this bossy annoyance if you were to reflect on the memories you spoke to me about and if you were to spend more time in the garden and with your friends.

I also wondered about Mary and what she might say to you. There are lots of questions in this letter. We can talk about them the next time we meet. I would be interested to know if you have noticed other times you are free from 'the annoyance'?

Coral

Second letter

Dear Jane

It was an honour to read your writings. I really liked the story about you buying your first home and how you made changes to the home and the garden. You spoke of the changes to the home and the garden as a way to express yourself. Your house and garden story also had me wondering if you have given any thought to how you made these changes, and how they fit with your life goals, dreams and aspirations now.

You mentioned that you have been learning to paint. Do you find this is one way you can express yourself in your new home? Or have you discovered other ways to express yourself since moving to the residential facility?

I was struck by your ability to develop ways to break free of 'the annoyance'. Today you said, 'I am getting there'. You said 'it is a slow progress but I know I can make it'. This had me reflecting on each of our sessions and of all the stories you have shared with me – of how you have managed to 'make it' throughout your life. I reflected on your stories of sadness and pleasure, of happiness and of joy and on how sometimes the life struggles have been quite overwhelming.

The stories that stand out for me are the stories of your long list of achievements, and of how you have always striven to bring up your family in a loving and respectful home. You spoke about respect and how you have noticed that respect is missing in the environment you now live. You mentioned how you would like to 'introduce respect' into the lives of the other residents and that you have been visiting your neighbours, always respecting their privacy and listening to their life stories.

When I left you today you told me that you had set yourself some tasks. One of them was to continue to get out of your room each day and pay a respectful visit to other people in the nursing home. You also said that your daughter had been asking you to go to go away with her for the weekend and you really wanted to go but 'the annoyance' may stop you. I noticed how you have begun to make plans for your life again – this took me by surprise! I also remembered you saying that your family and staff at the nursing home have noticed changes in you and have commented on how you are getting out of you room more. Is going on the weekend away the next step for you?

Jane, I noticed today that you are no longer letting 'the annoyance' overwhelm you and that you are experiencing a sense of freedom. I have noticed how hard you have worked to gain back the freedom.

You told me you will continue to write stories in your secret book because you have noticed the stories stop 'the annoyance' from playing tricks.

Now you have so much planned for your lifestyle, I am wondering if you need to see me so often. Next week you can let me know your thoughts on completing our sessions and if you have had any thoughts on how you might like to finish our visits.

Coral

Shortly after sending this letter I presented Jane with a Certificate of Achievement in Breaking Free From Annoyance.

Conclusion

It has become evident through conversations with Julie, Marge, Jane and other older women who were sexually abused as children, that many are struggling with issues of shame, loss of identity and social isolation. Too often these women speak of blaming themselves for the abuse they have experienced. And yet, these women are survivors with much wisdom and knowledge to share with others. This is wisdom and knowledge about pride, about respect, about special memories and relationships.

My hope is that we will continue to find ways to acknowledge the skills and survivor strategies of these women and that we will find ways to share these between women. We have recently initiated a group for older women to speak together about the preferred stories of their lives.

Writing this paper is another step in sharing these women's knowledges. It is also a step towards breaking the silence that for some of these women has lasted for longer than half a century.

Acknowledgements

I would like to thank David Denborough and Cheryl White for encouraging me with this project and Susan Phillips Reece from Southern Women's Community Health Centre, who helped me to develop ideas. I also acknowledge the older women who consult with me for the way they are strongly challenging the dominant stories of their lives and are now learning ways to live out their life's hopes and dreams. The writings of Amanda Kamsler (1998) and Michael White (1995) have also inspired my work in this area.

Notes

This paper was originally published in *Gecko: a journal of deconstruction and narrative ideas in therapeutic practice*, 2001 No.3. Republished here with permission.

The names of people concerned and the details of their stories have been altered to preserve confidentiality.

1. Coral works as a community worker with the Aged Care and Housing Group Inc in Adelaide, South Australia. Coral can be contacted c/o ACH Group Inc, Gordon Street Glenelg, South Australia.

References

Kamsler, A. 1998: 'Her-story in the making: Therapy with women who were sexually abused in childhood.' In White, C. & Denborough, D. (eds): *Introducing Narrative Therapy: A collection of practice-based writings.* Adelaide: Dulwich Centre Publications.

White, M. 1995: 'Naming abuse and breaking from it's effects.' An interview with Michael White by Chris McLean. In White, M.: *Re-Authoring Lives: Interviews and Essays* (chapter 4). Adelaide: Dulwich Centre Publications.

6.

Women's outrage and the pressure to forgive

Working with the survivors of childhood sexual abuse

from an interview with

Jussey Verco[1]

Because of the ways in which forgiveness is spoken about in the broader Christian-influenced culture and also in the mental health field, survivors of childhood sexual abuse are often placed under strong pressure to forgive the person who perpetrated abuse against them. Many women report that when they have accessed a group or counselling, that there has been an emphasis on forgiving the perpetrator and that this step is seen as necessary for healing.

As a worker, I am conscious that everyone goes through their own unique process in relation to coming to terms with the effects of sexual abuse. For a small number of women with whom I have worked, forgiveness *has* played an important part in their healing process and for them, the pressure to forgive may not have negative consequences. It may have been a process of their own choosing.

However, for most women with whom I've worked, the pressure to forgive can be oppressive. For many women survivors, there has been no acknowledgement of guilt or even of any wrongdoing by the person who perpetrated the abuse. In many situations the women have not been believed or have been viewed as in some ways culpable for the abuse to which they were subjected. Many women survivors have had significantly negative experiences when they have tried to inform their families of the abuse that occurred. For women in these situations, who form the majority of child sexual abuse survivors, questions of forgiveness are distant considerations.

When forgiveness is not something they feel they can grant, the pressure to forgive can result in these women judging themselves harshly because of their 'inability' to 'let go', to 'move on' and 'to forgive'. They can be invited into believing that they are 'bad' or 'evil'. A sense of shame about their ways of surviving abuse can then compound the effects of abuse with which they are already struggling.

The pressure for women to forgive can be placed in the broader context of societal attitudes towards women and anger in western culture. Within western culture, there are strong proscriptions about women and anger. When women express anger and outrage they can be at risk of being viewed as crazy, selfish, out of control and/or dangerous. Women are not 'supposed' to be angry and many women who have survived childhood sexual abuse know that there are very real risks in expressing their rage. Many of the women who attend the groups that we facilitate have in the past been subjected to a range of experiences, including:

being given psychiatric diagnosis, placed on medication, had their children taken away from them, and/or have even been detained in psychiatric hospitals. And some of these women believe that their expressions of anger and rage contributed to these experiences.

At the same time, in relation to experiences of childhood sexual abuse, women have often been recruited into blaming themselves for the abuse that occurred. There are numerous discourses that are still prevalent that locate the responsibility for sexual abuse with the survivors of this abuse rather than with the perpetrators. In this context, women's anger and outrage can be crucial in justly delegating responsibility for abuse. Survivors' outrage and an appreciation that the abuse was not their responsibility are inextricably linked. To deny women the right to feel outraged, to pressure them to forgive, is all too often to contribute to a sense of self-blame. This can further perpetuate abuse via systems abuse.

When working with women, we name these broader social factors. We talk together about the cultural beliefs surrounding women and anger and the impact that these beliefs have had on their lives. In these conversations, many women have spoken about how attempts to deny their outrage have been attempts to deny their history, to deny their experience, to deny their truth of what has occurred to their own bodies, to their lives.

Unpacking outrage

Rather than placing pressure on women to forgive, or assume that forgiveness is a prerequisite to healing, I am far more interested in acknowledging and honouring the justifiable outrage that many survivors of abuse express. Far from implying that this outrage is somehow an obstacle to forgiveness and therefore an impediment to healing, I am more interested in exploring what this outrage is a testimony to. What does this outrage speak to? What does it mean about the values the woman may hold about her life, about the rights of children to be safe and treated with respect? About the ways in which people should relate to each other?

In working with survivors of childhood sexual abuse, both in individual counselling and in group contexts, we invite women to talk about their justifiable outrage. Having done so, women often take the opportunity to share stories that may otherwise go unspoken.

Some women describe how they can be almost overtaken with a sense of outrage, and/or consumed by a sense of anger because of the effects of childhood sexual abuse. In these circumstances, anger may be taking up more space in the woman's life than she wants it to. Through the use of externalising conversations, the woman may state that she wants to move on from this anger, or perhaps that she wants to lessen its influence in her life, and to find an effective way of expressing and dealing with this anger. It may be that the woman sees the overwhelming nature of her anger as in some way a legacy of the power of the abuse that she wishes to reduce. Some women report that they realised that the outrage and anger that they feel is powerfully affecting their own life, while at the same time having no impact on the life of the perpetrator of the abuse.

I recall one woman some years ago who came to our group and mentioned that she'd like to talk about anger. When we enquired as to why this was something she wished to discuss, she explained that she was having nightmares in which she was doing terrible things to the person who perpetrated the sexual abuse against her. She had never talked about these nightmares with anybody before but she realised they were expressions of her outrage.

We asked her questions about her outrage, about what it represented, and what it meant to her. This woman was able to identify that her anger and outrage had been 'warning bells' for her, that told her when something was wrong, that her rights were being violated in some way. She identified that her current outrage was a declaration that an injustice had happened to her, and that she was concerned that further injustices were still occurring. In talking more about these warning bells and this woman's outrage, we unpacked how these were linked to certain principles and beliefs that she holds about the rights of children, about justice, about love, integrity, respect and honesty. In this way, far from outrage being seen as some hindrance to healing, we are interested in acknowledging the ways in which women's outrage is linked to the ethics by which they wish to live.

When this woman who had had the nightmares came back the following week, she said to us, 'I've been thinking a lot about our previous conversation. All of my life I've been so ashamed of the incredible outrage that I have felt in relation to what was done to me. I have kept this outrage secret and it's made me feel terrible about who I am. But now, I realise I should have been even more outraged! What he had done to me was outrageous. I should have been hopping mad and letting it out. Until now I haven't had a place to talk about this outrage, and I think this has led to my nightmares. I want to talk with you all more about what to do with this rage.'

As is our common practice, we then discussed ways in which women could express their outrage and anger: ways that will not hurt the women themselves or other people. One woman spoke about writing down expressions of her rage with a texta on toilet paper and then flushing these down the toilet. Other women develop rituals in which they write on paper and then burn the words, while other women may choose to smash plates in the backyard, or dance vigorously to their favourite music.

For some women, expressions of outrage include exploring ways of calling to account the person who perpetrated abuse against them. For the vast majority of women, this will not involve a formal legal process. The criminal justice system in general terms does not work for the survivors of childhood sexual abuse. If they wish to call the perpetrator to account in some way, alternative methods usually need to be arranged. For some women, this may involve directly confronting the person who perpetrated abuse against them – either in person or by writing them a letter.

For many survivors, directly confronting the person who perpetrated abuse against them is not an option as the perpetrator may still deny the childhood sexual abuse, may not be able to be located, or may even be dead. Women also need to weigh up potential safety issues for themselves if considering directly confronting the perpetrator. Other women may decide that they wish to express their outrage and the values their outrage represents by supporting other women survivors and/or taking some form of social action around the issue of childhood sexual abuse.

In these ways, rather than talking about forgiveness, we talk much more about women's justifiable outrage and how this outrage can lead to meaningful action. I think this is a beautiful and powerful way by which women can have their sense of injustice acknowledged.

Forgiving oneself

As I mentioned above, survivors of childhood sexual abuse have often been recruited into believing that they were somehow responsible for the abuse they experienced. This is a potent recipe for self-hate and self-loathing. This experience can be better understood when located within broader cultural practices. Patriarchal culture commonly locates women as the centre of problems in families. Blame is laid at women's feet in relation to most family issues. This means, that in working with survivors, we are often engaged in conversations to free women from the grips of self-blame. In some ways this can be seen as a process of self-forgiveness.

There are a number of factors of critical importance in this process. First of all, the women need to be believed, for their experience to be honoured and respected. I can't emphasise enough how significant this is. Just about every woman with whom I have worked has not been believed when she first disclosed her experiences of abuse. This initial disbelief often has a significant impact upon a woman's sense of self-worth. When a child is not only subject to abuse, but is then not believed about this abuse, their sense of identity and their sense of entitlement to respect or care, can be greatly diminished.

The second crucial factor relates to honouring the acts of resistance in which these women engaged when they were children. We seek to create a context in which women can begin to tell and re-tell the stories of how as children they sought safety, or how they resisted, or how they ran away. While this can be difficult for survivors to engage with at first, when the stories begin to be told and acknowledged, women start to get a different sense of themselves. They begin to see themselves in a different light. No longer do they see themselves as a person who was solely victimised by the abuse, or as a person who in some way colluded with the abuse. Instead they begin to acknowledge that as children they actively tried, in the ways available to them, to resist what they were being subjected to.

These stories need not be grand stories of resistance. For instance, they might consist of the times when she climbed the tallest tree in the backyard and stayed there until she was forced to come down. They might be stories of the times when she sat on the back fence for hours upon hours; or when she climbed to the roof; or ran away; or used her imagination to climb through the cracks in the wall. Or they might be stories about how she used to disassociate whilst her body was being subjected to sexual abuse so that her spirit wasn't present. When women begin to re-tell these stories and they are acknowledged as containing survival skills and knowledges, it can make a profound difference to how they understand themselves. Realising that they had engaged in some process of trying to keep themselves safe can enable women to contemplate what could be called 'self-forgiveness'. They are able to acknowledge that they had not agreed to the abuse happening and that they really had tried to stop it or to seek help.

Sharing these stories with an audience of other women survivors can also be transformative. This seems especially true for women who had previously understood their survival strategies in negative ways. For instance, many women who disassociated at the time of abuse have had concerns that this reflects that they were somehow 'crazy' or 'messed up'. When they hear from other women who did the same thing, who honour the child's ability to care for herself, and who understand this as a survival strategy, it can be very liberating.

I recall one particular woman who when we first started a conversation in the group about survival knowledges, said, 'I didn't do anything'. When we began to talk together about things that she had found hard as a child, she told us that she had been a tomboy. There were about twelve women present in the group on that day, and as we went around the table every single woman replied that she too had been a tomboy! Of course, we then had a discussion about what this could possibly mean and the women came up with some fantastic reflections. Perhaps it had meant that even as little girls they had somehow worked out that boys were less likely to be subjected to sexual abuse. Or perhaps that they had cut their hair and worn boys' clothes in order to appear less conventionally attractive. Or perhaps they had thought that if they hung out with the boys and something untoward began to happen, then the boys might keep them safe. Or perhaps they'd worked out that boys simply had more fun! One woman reflected on how the games that boys played, such as riding bikes, were much more appealing to her than the games the girls played such as 'mummies and daddies'. This particular woman would have found it terrifying to be playing a game in which you were supposed to enact what mummies and daddies did. As women shared these experiences, there was an amazing ripple around the table as they recognised their childhood acts of resistance.

As women speak about their childhood acts of resistance and ways that they endeavoured to either keep themselves safe or make some stand against what was happening, it takes away the power of 'self-blame'. The woman who at the beginning of the meeting had said that she hadn't done anything to resist came back the next week and said, 'I've been smiling all week long knowing that, yes, I did, I really did try to make some kind of stand'.

Externalising conversations and migrations of identity

In enabling women to break free from self-blame, we have also found it helpful to engage in externalising conversations in relation to the 'voice of abuse'. By externalising 'the voice of abuse', there becomes a much greater chance for women to separate themselves from the thoughts and understandings of themselves which the abuse experience recruited them into. Throughout our conversations we can ask questions about 'the voice of abuse', its effects and the ways in which it has been and can be resisted. In some situations we also externalise 'the voice of patriarchy' as this assists in making visible the many prescriptions that these women need to deal with in relation to who they should and shouldn't be, and what they can and can't do.

As the 'voice of abuse' and the 'voice of patriarchy' are externalised and as dominant ideas associated with childhood sexual abuse are deconstructed and challenged, it becomes more possible for the women to embrace qualities and traits of which they can be proud. As women break free from self-blame it becomes easier for them to identify what they appreciate about themselves. Women make statements such as: 'I actually have a kind heart', or 'I stand by my word', or 'I'm a good friend'. We are then able to spend time in building on these alternative understandings and finding stories that support them.

This process of moving from negative ideas about identity to more positive ones can be a long process and can have ups and downs. Breaking away from negative ideas about your identity and creating a new, more positive sense of yourself, involves moving from the known into the unknown. Once women have become freed up from self-blame and self-hatred and before they have become re-grounded in a positive sense of identity, they go through a betwixt and between stage which has both wonderful and terrifying aspects. Everything that they once thought they knew becomes questioned. Many women have told us that as they step into new understandings of who they are, they learn to say 'no' to various things that once they would have always agreed to do. This has meant that along the way some women have lost contact with friends and even family.

In our experience, mapping out this migration of identity can be of great assistance (see White 1995). We find it important to predict that women will have times when the voice of abuse will lash back at them, as well as times when they will feel stronger and more connected to good ideas about themselves. By predicting the hard times, when difficulties do arise the women realise that they are not going crazy or they have not gone back to square one and instead can recall the ideas and strategies that had been prepared for just such occasions. This can connect women with their own abilities to care for themselves.

As women move through this process of healing they make predictions and forecasts and plot their journey along the way. At the end of each session we give women a map and get them to take it home and to plot where they think they are in terms of their migration of identity. These maps are then constantly available to be consulted, reviewed and amended.

Last words

Migrations of identity in relation to the effects of sexual abuse can be long journeys. And yet over the years, women have demonstrated time and again how these migrations can be made. Having others around to assist in the process, making preparations for difficult times, having justifiable outrage as a respected companion, and *not* being pressured to forgive, all make the process of reclaiming one's life from the effects of sexual abuse considerably more manageable.

In the process, many survivors also make significant contributions to supporting other women and creating greater awareness about the issue of childhood sexual abuse. Routinely, these journeys of healing are accompanied by deliberate, creative and courageous acts aimed towards ensuring greater safety for all our children. These acts are often the result of women's anger, women's outrage. What better use of outrage could there possibly be?

Acknowledgements

The ideas in this paper are by no means mine alone. They have been shaped by my conversations with women survivors of childhood sexual abuse and other workers over the last seven years.

Notes

This paper was originally published in the International Journal of Narrative Therapy & Community Work, 2002 No.1. Republished here with permission.

1. The interview from which this paper was created was conducted by staff writer, David Denborough. Jussey can be contacted c/o Dulwich Centre Publications.

Reference

White, M. 1995: 'Naming abuse and breaking from its effects.' An interview by Christopher McLean in White, M., *Re-Authoring Lives: Interviews & essays.* Adelaide: Dulwich Centre Publications.

7.

Seeking safety and acknowledgement

Women who have experienced domestic violence

by

WOWSafe[1]

Women of the West for Safe Families (WOWSafe) is an organisation of women in Adelaide, South Australia, who have personally survived men's violence in the home and now campaign in order to prevent it in the lives of others. This paper, which was constructed from a series of interviews, discusses some of the complexities of forgiveness in relation to domestic violence.

Times when we did forgive in the past

Some of the women spoke about the times when they were still in relationships with their partners who were violent, and the times in which they did forgive. They spoke about how the question of forgiveness has been a complex one in their lives.

- *Some years ago I took him back on two occasions and forgave him. The Police nearly hung me for this. I was seen as unstable. It was no matter of congratulating me for having the guts to try and get my marriage to work. There was no pat on the back. Instead, it was 'whatever happens to you now is your fault, you took him back'. They turned on me something terrible. So, on top of my other troubles I then felt I had the police as enemies.*

- *If you do forgive, and take your partner back, it affects all your relationships. I remember walking back into the social services and, while they had been all friendly the first time I went in, the next time they were stand-offish. I knew I was being punished for having forgiven my partner, for having taken him back. They obviously thought that I would do this again and again. And most women do. Most women take their partners back several times before they can finally leave. This is a common part of the experience of trying to leave a domestic violence situation. I know this must be hard for people to understand, but it would help if we weren't punished for trying to find our way through very complex situations.*

- *While we were still living together I would forgive and forgive and forgive, but I cannot forgive anymore. Other women in my community believe that I should keep on forgiving. But I cannot. My advice to other women is to look after yourself. You cannot keep forgiving for too long.*

Hazards of forgiveness

Women spoke a lot about some of the hazards of forgiving when you are in a situation of violence.

When we forget we put ourselves in danger. *For a long time I would just forget about the violence that my partner directed towards me and this put me at risk. A lot of us do this, perhaps out of fear that we are not going to be able to meet anyone else. In hindsight, this kind of forgetting or forgiving did not take a great deal of strength. It was the easy but dangerous option. What took more strength was to be able to think and say, 'I am not guilty and this has to stop'. That's what took strength, that's what was so hard.*

Forgiving and forgetting. *After leaving my husband everyone was telling me to 'just get on with my life' and so I tried to forgive and forget. But there came a time when it all came smashing back down. My mind, my spirit was telling me, 'hang on, everything is not rosy and peachy. Something is really wrong here.' That's how I ended up coming into this group. I needed to talk with others about all that had happened. I couldn't just get on with life without coming to terms with the effects of the violence on every part of my life.*

To forgive is to risk further violence. Various women spoke about how, in their experience, to forgive is to risk further violence: *I'm scared of using the word forgiveness, because in my experience you get shit on if you do forgive over and over. So many times women forgive and forget and expose themselves to more violence. So often perpetrators look at forgiveness as a weakness – 'she's a sucker', 'I've won her', 'I can get away with that one', 'she's a pushover'.*

I still have to be wary and alert. I'm having to move house because once he is released, everyone says that he will head straight for me. He will knock on the door and say 'hello darling'. He doesn't believe he has done anything wrong. I still have to be guarded against him. I can't forget, I can't forgive, I have to be guarded.

He got something over me when I forgave him. *In the groups I went to some years ago I was taught over and over again that I must forgive in order to get on with my life. And so I sat down with my partner and I actually forgave him for what he had done to me and what he had said to me over the years. Since that day he has continually repeated the things that he did before I forgave him, and this has made me a much harder person. I am just so sorry that I did forgive him* *then, because I will never forgive him again. I just can't. I feel he got something over me when I forgave him and it's hurt even more.*

Obstacles to forgiveness

Some of the women talked about how they found forgiveness not to be possible in their particular situations.

When he won't admit that what he did was wrong. *My husband will never admit that what he did was wrong and it's hard to forgive someone in this sort of situation. How can I forgive if I am the only one holding onto the fact that what he did was wrong. If I let go of that, if I forgive, then what do I have left? I do not even have my reality. What I know happened will suddenly be believed by no-one, not even myself. I don't think you can forgive someone if they don't even know what they did to you. There has to be acknowledgement before there can be a moving on.*

Our partners rarely forgive us for seeking safety. Other women spoke about the irony that often it is their partners who never forgave them once they took some action to protect themselves from the violence: *After I took action to protect myself and my children my partner never forgave me. He never forgave me and believed from that day on that I was 'treacherous'. I was 'treacherous' because I'd had the courage to run away with my kids to try to make it safe. How often does a man in a domestic violence situation forgive a woman? Usually they continue the blame and the scorn forever, and yet it is they who abused us, not the other way around.*

I remember my partner at all hours of the morning saying, 'I'll forgive you if you apologise for calling the police'.

Forms of forgiveness

Some of the women present spoke about how they had found certain aspects of the concept of forgiveness to be helpful, and they were very clear in articulating which aspects these were.

Forgiveness as choosing to live without hatred. *Holding onto resentment can make you old and ugly. In this way forgiveness can help to get rid of the hatred and the stress inside yourself. It can be freeing. I've found this for me and my family. It isn't about him so much, as about allowing us to live life without bitterness.*

Forgiveness and understanding. *At times I have needed to forgive in order to get on with my own life. I may not forgive him completely, but I've come to forgive in the sense of 'there must be a reason why he did this'. Thinking about this has made me acknowledge what happened to him as a child. This doesn't mean that he isn't accountable for what he did to me, but somehow it helps me to understand and to get on with my own life.*

Understanding how it happened. *Understanding how it happened and what might have contributed to him acting in those ways has been helpful. It's been a part of separating myself from the effects of the abuse. It's not about excusing him, it's about understanding. For me this helps.*

Forgiving him as a person, but not what he did. *I can forgive him as a person, but I could never forgive what he did to me or the boys. I can forgive him for the fact that he is a person who made mistakes – as I am. But that's as far as it goes. I don't want to have to sit here today and say I feel good about him. I don't.*

Compensation. *To me it was an acknowledgement when I received compensation and it enabled me to move on. I don't know if I forgive him, but I no longer hold a grudge.*

Questions of honour. Women from non-Anglo cultures spoke of some of the complexities of trying to come to terms with experiences of violence when the community you come from is also affected by the effects of racism. These same women also spoke about specific cultural traditions of honour that they try to call upon even though they themselves have been dishonoured. They spoke about how this to them was related to the concept of forgiveness: *'I want to be honourable even though my husband was dishonourable. I want to live an honourable life so that my child can learn how to become a good person.'*

Parenting without malice. *There are many ways of showing generosity that aren't necessarily about forgiveness, and some of these include how we choose to raise our children. We can choose not to put hatred into our children's heads and hearts. We can choose to raise them without malice or bitterness. To heap hatred onto children deprives them of the chance to make up their own minds, make their own relationships. We don't have to incite them against their fathers, no matter what these men may have done to us. There is a particular beauty when mothers find ways of relating to their kids that are different, that are not about violence or anger or bitterness. Despite all that we may be carrying around in our hearts, we can still be good, loving mothers.*

Relating to our children

In talking about forgiveness, one of the significant topics that was discussed concerned women's children. Various mothers in the group spoke about the complexities they experience in relation to raising their children. There was a heartfelt exchange between two mothers that is included here:

My son has been determined never to hit back, to never be like his dad but he is finding that the bullies target him now. They know that he'll run away rather than hit back. Some of the teachers are now telling him 'to stand up for himself'. He won't bully back because I've taught him that physical and verbal abuse is all wrong. It is really hard.

I taught my kids that if you can walk away you walk away. But I also taught them that if there comes a time when you've got to stand up for yourself and if you have to hit back then hit back – but do everything else in your power first. I couldn't tell my young kids not to protect themselves. They are all grown up now, and it worked for them. You've got to teach people how to draw the line. Well that's what we did.

I agree with you, but when I then did try to convey this to my son, he said, 'No, I don't want to.' He has a beautiful nature, and he said, 'No mum, that's not right. I'd rather go and find a teacher.' He just refuses to be violent and I love him for it.

Well I reckon you've done all you can do. You have given him a choice and he is making his own decisions now. He sounds like a beautiful young man.

Other mothers also told stories about the effects of violence on their children:

I have a son who is now 28 and he can still remember my husband beating me. He's never forgiven his father because he is old enough to remember what his father did to me. He's got so much hate in him. He can't go to counselling and talk about it. He just lashes out and smashes things. Every situation is different. In those days there was no such thing as a refuge. There was nowhere to go. I find it hard to know how to help my son now. This is a bigger concern to me than thinking about forgiveness.

Another mother discussed how raising her young children means she has to think about forgiveness and what she believes:

Now that I am a parent, I have had to learn about forgiveness. It is hard for me to hold onto hatred for people who have treated me badly in the past when I am trying to teach my young child about how forgiveness is important. Sometimes it feels like I am living a double life. I guess I am looking at the way I was raised in a religious perspective in which forgiveness is so important for the soul. I look at this and believe it is right to teach children not to have so much anger and hatred. But at the same time, I struggle with my own sense of anger.

Other considerations

In talking about forgiveness a number of other issues were also discussed. These have been included here:

Protection. Many women spoke of a lack of confidence in others, including the justice system, in protecting them from the men who have been violent towards them. This makes a considerable difference in terms of considerations of forgiveness. If women are still at risk of violence, their primary aim is to protect their life and the lives of their children. Women talked about a wide range of ways in which they try to protect themselves and their children – skills of evasion, of support from others, skills of flight, physical strength, carrying weapons, changing names and identities, constant vigilance over one's own life and one's children, and many others.

It is impossible to forget. *I may be able to forgive but it is impossible to forget. The colours, songs, and even foods can bring back the memories. Whether or not I forgive, I always remember. I don't mean I remember in a bad way, but things just come back. For instance, one evening I might be aching in the bone that he broke, and think of the events that led to this. That's what I mean. It is impossible to forget. Forgiveness doesn't stop the memories coming back, it doesn't take away the hurts.*

Revenge. Some women spoke of the ways in which they had been tempted to, or even had tried to, find people who would cause harm to those who had been violent towards them. Usually these attempts were unsuccessful: *I have long hoped for a day when the tables would be turned – where my husband would be in the position of having to decide whether he would forgive or forget. But I will not see that day.*

Relationships with our mothers. Various women also talked a lot about their relationships with their mothers. Many of the women had experienced violence as children, often at the hands of the male partners of their mothers, and spoke of the difficulties this brought into their relationships with their mums. Some of the women spoke about how they have tried to forgive their mums for their inaction, how they've tried to understand how it all took place. Other women spoke about how this isn't a possibility for them and how they are dedicating their lives to caring for their children in ways that they did not experience.

Not something to be forced. All the women agreed that forgiveness is not something that should be forced: *There's nobody in this room whose partner has really acknowledged the effects of their violence, shown genuine remorse and been really concerned about not abusing power again. If our partners had done this, then maybe forgiveness would flow naturally. Then again, maybe it wouldn't. But whatever the case, forgiveness isn't something we should have to force. I don't think we should have to forgive in order to feel good about ourselves.*

I don't think forgiveness can happen until the violence and abuse has ended and the perpetrators are taking some responsibility for this violence.

The broader question of White Australia apologising to Indigenous Australia

WOWSafe consists of women from a diversity of cultural backgrounds. On the day of this discussion, a well-respected Aboriginal woman, Dawn, was present and her presence enabled conversation about a range of issues that otherwise would not have been possible. Over the past years in Australia there has been considerable discussion about whether non-Indigenous Australia ought to apologise to Indigenous Australia in relation to past injustices. National Sorry Days have taken place in which hundreds of thousands of Australians have marched to express their regret and sorrow for the events of the past. As ideas about reconciliation and sorry and apology have been, and continue to be, a significant part of the national consciousness, this discussion on forgiveness touched on these broader issues. More specifically, the non-Aboriginal women were very interested to hear Dawn's perspective on these issues. One woman therefore asked, 'Dawn, can I ask you what it means to you for white Australians to say sorry?' This was Dawn's response:

When it comes from politicians, 'Sorry' is just a word to me, but to see the people march on Sorry Day, that meant a lot. To see the white people and black people walking together and dancing together, to see their sincerity, this was significant to me. I know that some people are really sorry. I've had people burst into tears when they have heard certain stories. When people have had the chance to know about certain things that happened in my life, for example having been through the institutions, they couldn't wait to hold me and tell me with tears that they were sorry, even though they were not personally responsible. That's been significant to me.

The politicians, though, I think their time would be better spent making sure that there was water and sewerage for the Aboriginal settlements. There need to be acts of sorry. And there need to be acts of acknowledgement. We still hear people talk about the difficult conditions that some groups are experiencing in different parts of the world. I don't want us to forget about those people, but Aboriginal people are still suffering right here in this country. I'm on a Bringing Them Home Committee and we have been talking about what would be the most appropriate acts of Sorry from the Government. For most of us, what we would like is to be educated in our language and in our law and in our religion – everything that we missed out on as a child.

When you are taken away and placed in white institutions, you don't belong to them, you don't belong to anybody. We'd like to be given back the opportunity to remake our identities, to relearn our language. And we're talking about the young and the old – the 14 year-olds, the 16 years-olds, the 60 year-olds. That's what acts of Sorry would look like to me. I don't know whether that would enable forgiveness, but it's what a good future looks like to me.

Notes

This paper was created from an interview conducted by Dulwich Centre Publications' staff writer David Denborough, and was originally published in the *International Journal of Narrative Therapy & Community Work*, 2002 No.1. Republished here with permission.

1. WOWSafe can be contacted c/o The Parks Community Health Centre, Trafford St, Angle Pk SA 5010, Australia.

8.

Creating respectful relationships in the name of the Latino family:

A community approach to domestic violence

the work of
Alberto Colorado
Pamela Montgomery
Jesús Tovar

We feel strongly that in order to understand domestic violence within the Latino community, and to work respectfully on the issue, the broader violence and oppression experienced by Latin Americans in North America needs to be acknowledged. We believe that violence within Latino families needs to be seen from a perspective that encompasses the many manifestations of social violence and injustice.

Most conventional therapeutic approaches that address domestic violence have been formulated by persons with economic stability and social privilege. Because of this, we have found that they are often inappropriate and/or disrespectful to Latino communities and Latino ways of being. Many attempts to address domestic violence can make Latino people feel more estranged from their own culture. Such attempts can contribute to weakening the Latino family and increasing division within the community, rather than strengthening the family and building community unity.

Latin American people are consistently invited to feel that Latino culture is in some way inherently violent and that the solution to this violence lies in western ways of being. Approaches to domestic violence all too often ignore the histories of violence that Latino people have experienced and ignore the elements of Latin American culture that have always stood against violence. The way in which these cultural traditions have been displaced due to histories of colonisation and dislocation is also generally ignored. There is a pervasive view that the only way to deal with domestic violence is through adherence to dominant white western ways. Some of these ways, such as 'assertiveness' training for women or notions of 'open communication', have been identified by Latino people as potentially placing Latina women at a greater risk of violence, as well as disrespecting Latino ways of speaking and relating.

Within this context we have tried to develop an alternative approach that honours the cultural backgrounds and current experiences of Latin Americans. We are seeking ways of reducing violence between Latino people that promote community unity, strengthen Latino families and regenerate Latino culture.

Community meetings – an inclusive approach

The forums for our work are community meetings which we facilitate. By amplifying private conversations to include families, friends, teachers or any others who may enrich the process, we make a political decision to address domestic violence as a community issue. At the same time, an audience of community members becomes available to witness and authenticate the construction of narratives that foster respectful relations (see White & Epston 1990, p.191).

Within Latin American cultures there is a great diversity of ways of being. Cultural histories including both pro-violence and pro-respect messages can be found. We suggest that cultural messages that foster or inhibit violence can be taken into account in community work on domestic violence. We propose the reclaiming of enriching cultural stories that promote respect among family members. We seek to create a context in which the liberatory elements of Latino culture can be built upon to foster the creation of respectful relationships.

Conceptual elements of the workshop

The conceptual elements described here serve as guidelines for our workshops rather than as rigid, chronological steps. We use the elements flexibly in order to adapt to the group and/or create variety within a series of workshops.

- The joining process.
- Externalising conversations.
- Tracing the influence of problems on the lives and relationships of persons.
- Using the culture as a transforming agent.
- Tracing the influence of persons on problems.
- Translating narratives into concrete steps.
- Closing ceremony.

The joining process

> *... Let us remember scenes of harmony from our places of origin, scenes
> that fortify us in this strange and different world. Let us remember the
> landscape and the people of our native lands, memories that support us
> as we struggle to live in a new society. Not everything was left behind
> when we crossed the border. We bring skills and strengths, traditions and
> love. We bring commitments to family and community that help us work
> toward lives without violence. We can free ourselves from words and
> actions that destroy what we value... We already have with us customs
> and knowledges that can be seeds for a better future. Let us build upon
> our cultural strengths and empower ourselves in the name of the family.*

We begin our workshops with a cultural ceremony called a *ch'ulel* (which means
'spirit' in the Mayan language). We use the *ch'ulel* to welcome the participants
and to facilitate the joining process. All persons form a circle to create an
atmosphere of connection with each other and with their shared Latino heritage.
Jesús or Alberto leads this opening *ch'ulel*.

The playing of Latin American music promotes a spirit of belonging to
common cultural roots. Cultural symbols or objects (such as musical instruments,
icons and/or native foods) enhance the sense of identification with the Latin
American heritage. Information and narratives read by one of the facilitators link
persons with their past, with the purpose of the workshop and with future
commitments to homes without violence.

After the *ch'ulel*, participants are invited to introduce themselves and
share a quality that they like about themselves and that serves to fortify their
families. Facilitators and participants write their quality on a piece of paper and
put the paper in a basket which is then placed in the centre of the circle. The
written qualities represent the people's strengths which will help them create
alternatives to the narratives of domestic violence.

Participants can also be asked to dedicate a life without violence to
someone in their lives, then write the name of this person and put the name into
the basket. As another alternative, they can write the name of someone from their
family or culture who has served as a role model for respectful rationships. In
these ways, participants are invited to join with their own skills and knowledges,

as well as with histories of respect within their own lives and the lives of their families and community.

The next step involves a joining of participants with the theme of the workshop. One member of our team reads a true story about a Latino family that is confronting violent beliefs and practices. Sharing the story opens space for the participants to identify with the members of the family. We have found that this identification produces a bridge between the participants and the theme of domestic violence. As discussed earlier, there are many restraints to overcome in order to create constructive conversations about domestic violence.

We have found that this process of joining creates an atmosphere which allows people to speak openly about a difficult subject. It creates a context in which participants can share thoughts, feelings and ideas about domestic violence through externalising conversations.

Externalising conversations

We have sought to find ways of overcoming the many factors that restrain conversations about domestic violence. One of the ways we have tried to do this is to invite externalising conversations that refuse to locate the problem within individuals and that instead invite the participants to join together to resist the problem.

Early on in the workshop Jesús or Alberto reads a story in the hope that it will open space for participants to then speak of their own experiences. The story is a short history of a Latino family.

We have noticed during the *ch'ulel* and the reading of the story that participants often respond *por el corazón* (through the heart). They are touched emotionally by what they hear and this contributes to a heightened awareness of the damaging effects of family violence. Through identifying with the protagonists of the story, participants begin to consider the ways in which violent practices have hurt their own lives and the lives of loved ones. In witnessing the heart-felt response of many participants to the *ch'ulel* and story, we as facilitators are put in touch with our own experiences and are reminded of our profound responsibility to work sensitively with this painful theme. We are reminded of our commitment to respect the life experiences and well-being of all participants.

After the reading of the story, the participants begin to share their responses to the story. The goal is not to promote censure of the family members in the story, but to continue developing an emotional identification with the effects of domestic violence on all concerned. This dynamic is considered essential for motivating participants to create alternative discourses and actions later in the workshop.

We then invite the participants to trace the influence of the problems on the family in the narrated story. They discuss how various beliefs, attitudes and strategies affect different areas of the family members' lives (home, work, school). The extent of domestic violence and its effects are articulated. As community member Carmen described to us: *Domestic violence includes not only physical blows but also yelling, insults and vulgar words.*

The participants are also invited, through the use of questions, to explore the elements within the story that promote violent practices and those which promote respectful relationships. This is the deconstruction phase of the narrative approach, a phase in which persons observe and analyse the stories which constitute their lives. We explore the participants' understanding of the links between violence and broader power relations. We ask questions concerning the cultural and social influences on the problem of domestic violence. With these questions, we try to offer the opportunity to talk about issues of gender, patriarchy, ethnicity, economic and/or social class, etc. As participants answer these questions, they explore the social messages that have informed and taught them about violent practices. They express many ideas about cultural and social factors that generate violent acts within families.

Through conversations about the story, participants are invited to consider how discourses on gender, ethnicity and immigration impact familial interactions and their life choices. We use the story to open conversations about the complex arena of beliefs, discourses and circumstances within which violent practices arise. Some of the themes that generally emerge from these discussions include:

- the personal, cultural and gendered narratives that justify violent acts,

- the pressure of First World policies and politics,

- the apparent lack of alternatives to violent acts due to racial and economic tensions,

- the misconception that violence is the only way to express frustrations,

- the misconception that violence is an effective means of controlling others,

- the loss of vision of the Latino family being a place for the well-being of its members.

In this part of the workshop, we have been greatly influenced by Alan Jenkins' work with men who abuse (1990). We are careful to avoid inviting the externalisation of problems such as 'violence' or 'aggression'. We are conscious that if we invite the externalisation of feelings and experiences like 'abuse' or 'temper', we might give the erroneous impression that those who abuse are not responsible for their behaviour. We instead encourage the externalisation of attitudes and ideas that seem to compel violence, such as a belief in patriarchy. We also externalise strategies used to subjugate persons, such as isolation, coercion, or economic deprivation. We ask questions about the factors that the participants see as fostering violent practices in their homes. Their views generally range over many areas. We work with the suggestions given by the community in ways that invite those perpetrating violence to take responsibility for this violence. We wish to find ways of acknowledging the experience and knowledge of the community, and begin a dialogue about the restraints we are up against in addressing violence without in any way justifying violent actions.

Factors that foster violent practices in our homes:

- Discrimination and racism.

- Patriarchal ideas about ways of being men: *'El machismo' promotes violence. A man says that he has the right to rule because he works. But if the woman works, the man continues to rule, even though she may earn more or he may not even be working.* (Carmen)

- Many expenses and bills.

- Lack of communication.

- Lack of understanding.

- Use of abusive words.

- Histories of violence: *I grew up with violence in my home. My father spoke little but abused with words, and my mother always used violence to discipline us.* (Raúl)

- Loneliness.

- Lack of money: *The economic situation affects me. I become desperate because there is never enough money. I am always worried.* (Lucia)

- Gang activities.

- Use of drugs and/or alcohol: *Violence appears in the presence of alcohol. Alcohol destroys the mind and the capacity to think.* (Carmen)

- Changes in the perception of gender roles.

- Parents and other loved ones living far away.

- Government politics and anti-immigration legislation.

- Difficulty adapting to a new culture and learning a new language.

- Violence in the broader society: *In my childhood I was in a position to observe a lot of violence, principally from abusive men. The violence was always accompanied by alcohol. Without the alcohol the family was different. Society itself is violent, music is violent, television is violent. The chain of misery continues to reproduce itself from generation to generation. When you get married you are not prepared to be a husband or wife.* (Victor)

These conversations have a number of effects. Firstly, they are an opportunity for community members to name and honour their experiences. They can then create alternative explanations for the violence within the Latino community than those often offered by the dominant culture – which, as described earlier, are often racist in their assumptions and effects.

Secondly, by collectively examining the many influences on people's lives, a context is created which tends to take from persons the burden of individual and familial blame. With the broader context to their lives acknowledged, participants are invited out of seeing their problems as private failures. Difficulties can be considered as aspects of a broad social structure, and the positive forces of the individual and family can be freed up to move forward. We have found that conversations which acknowledge the broader context tend to motivate persons to unite with others to change denigrating social systems.

Great care is needed in the facilitation of these conversations. We wish to honour the experiences of those within the community and to facilitate a sense of collective action, while not encouraging any individual participants to abdicate from their own personal responsibility to address violent acts which they may have committed. One way we have found through this dilemma is to explore the ways in which family members, influenced by social messages that justify violence and inequality, can lose sight of their responsibility to create respectful relationships.

We also need to take great care to ensure that, throughout these conversations (and throughout the workshop), the voices and experiences of those who have experienced violence are heard and honoured. We use a variety of methods to do this. We ask questions in large and small group settings. We divide participants into groups by gender with the other gender at times serving as a reflecting team. We divide participants into small groups with someone taking notes and then sharing what was said with the entire group. We create opportunities for expression through artistic means. In order to ensure that those who have been subjected to violence experience the workshop as helpful and respectful, we give participants the opportunity to give feedback, either verbally or through written comments, at the end of each workshop. We also call or visit participants afterwards to enquire about the real effects of the workshop on their lives.

One of our ongoing concerns involves how to invite participation in the various parts of the workshop while at the same time ensuring that people have the freedom to choose not to speak. We attempt to create an atmosphere in which persons never feel obligated to share ideas or experiences. We have heard from participants after workshops that they feel this is crucial. Several have told us that, for some women, it might compromise their safety at home if they spoke about their personal experiences.

With the broader context and influences named we move on to the next part of the workshop.

Tracing the influence of problems on the lives and relationships of persons

In the next stage of our workshops, we invite participants to trace the effects of the problem of domestic violence on their lives. As these effects become articulated in a communal space, it becomes more possible to protest or transform the problem. At this stage we ask questions that move into the domain of personal experience with familial violence. Many participants by this point are ready to share how they have been affected by violent narratives and practices. Members of our team and participants mutually develop an understanding of the experiences described in the participants' stories.

Together the facilitators and participants confront the reality of violence in the home. We explore the effects of aggressive displays of power and control through physical, mental and/or economic means. We explore the ways in which domestic violence profoundly affects the entire family, without denying the different responsibilities that different members have in addressing this violence (namely the different responsibilities that those who commit acts of violence have to redress and to ensure that no further harm occurs). The following themes often emerge from these discussions.

Feelings associated with violent practices in our homes:

- Tension.
- Hatred.
- Fear: *I'm afraid. My husband says that he doesn't want a relationship based on fear – that he recognises his mistakes. He asks for forgiveness. We try to avoid fighting, to separate and calm ourselves. We hardly talk because we don't want to end up fighting. We feel so distant from each other. He still says vulgar things and strikes things in the house. The children feel frightened too.* (Lucía, conversation, 1996)
- Anger: *Anger is like a monster – alcohol sets it free.* (Raúl)
- Lack of control.
- Feelings of failure and culpability.
- Sadness.

- Remorse.

- Frustration over coming to this country and not finding work in one's profession: *Frustration dominates all of us. It robs value from our lives.* (Lucía)

- Desperation over not achieving 'the American dream'.

This thorough exploration of the effects of the problem of domestic violence seeks to honour the experiences of those in the room. We have found that as participants who have perpetrated violence become more aware of the effects of this violence on the persons subjected to it, and as they become more aware of their own emotional response to the knowledge of these effects, they tend to take more responsibility for their actions. We have also found that an acknowledgment of the many effects of domestic violence opens the way for a later investigation of unique outcomes, moments and situations when persons have resisted or triumphed over violence and have built respectful relationships. Prior to this exploration, however, we endeavour to create a context in which liberatory Latino cultural traditions can be highlighted and drawn upon.

Using the culture as a transforming agent

The next section of the workshop is informed by our experiences and understandings of Latin American traditions. In our experience, the 'narrative approach' to therapy can fit well with Latin American cultural traditions and the Latin American world view. Central to Latin American culture is a strong oral tradition through which values, beliefs and knowledges are passed from one generation to the next. Cultural beliefs and traditions are often expressed in the form of stories or legends. Latin Americans, influenced by this story-telling tradition, tend to conceive of problems in the form of a story. Personal and collective stories are embedded in a holistic view of the world. Human beings are generally seen in relationship to each other and to other elements of the world. Physical, mental, emotional, behavioural and spiritual aspects of life are seen as interconnected rather than as separate. This holistic view relates well to an approach that integrates the different spheres of human experience and considers the multiple contexts of people's lives.

Similarly, we believe that the ethical parameters promoted by what has come to be known as 'narrative therapy', such as sensitivity to the relevant culture and a spirit of collaboration, offer hopeful possibilities for working with Latin American people. Our goal of using a narrative approach with Latin Americans is to create an appropriate cultural context in which the participants can formulate new descriptions of their lives and relationships. Based on a heightened awareness of cultural mores and dominant social narratives, we believe that this process can help persons act in more preferred and empowering ways. We believe that using 'narrative ways of working' to explore and honour Latino ways of being offers the potential for the transformation of lives.

Within Latino culture, both pro-violence and pro-respect messages can be found. We try to structure conversations in which participants can identify cultural narratives that support violence and those that alternatively support respectful relationships. We believe that this process makes respectful ways of relating more available for participants to take into their own lives and relationships. There are a number of ways we seek to create these conversations.

We present Latino culture as consisting of both alienating and affirming narratives, of discourses that promote, and of discourses that discourage violent acts. We have found it helpful at times to personify 'Latino culture' with the following sorts of questions:

• *If the culture could talk, what would it say about domestic violence?*

• *What would be its messages for and against violent strategies and practices?*

• *What would it invite us to say and do?*

Another method we have used at this point is to explore the messages in songs, proverbs and stories of the culture. As the participants share ideas, a team member makes two lists on a whiteboard: one list containing the pro-violence messages, and another containing the pro-respect messages. The idea is to clarify how cultural/social/political narratives support different discourses on domestic violence.

Two different outcomes from these conversations are common. Firstly, a sense of history is evoked and this serves as an acknowledgment of what the community is up against: *Violence has existed for generations since one's parents have been raised with physical blows. It is a chain that continues.* (Elizabeth)

Secondly, however, an alternative history begins to be unearthed – a history of cultural practices that stand against violence and that support respectful relationships.

I am from a town where everyone knew each other. This promoted respect. The people had more identity. They were interested in their homes, more respectful, more communicative. I learned to believe in communication to reach understanding and to solve problems by talking. (María)

Cultural distortions

What is also common within these discussions is an articulation of how Latino culture has become distorted in many ways by the dominant North American culture. At times these distortions have been referred to by participants as 'pseudo-culture'.

The pseudo-culture presented by the media creates models of vulgar, vain, 'macho' messages. The pseudo-culture views the woman as an object. She must be domesticated to be obedient and docile. When a girl is born, people become sad. The pseudo-culture does not respect a woman. (Victor)

It has been a liberating experience to explore these distortions of Latino culture and to invite participants to articulate the aspects of Latino culture that they value. These conversations have fostered a reclaiming of Latino identity and traditions from the distortions of the dominant North American culture. Two of the themes that often emerge when reclaiming Latino culture include 'respect' and 'dedication to the children'.

Authentic values are those that fortify the family with respect. (Raúl).

In our culture there is a strong dedication to the children. Everything that is done is based on them and their future. If we love our children, we should think of them and therefore not argue in front of them. We should talk things out and reflect. (Osvelia)

In this way a process is begun in which participants seek to separate pro-violence cultural messages, and the distortions of Latino culture made by the dominant culture, from pro-respect messages embedded within Latino cultural histories. To further this process, theatrical approaches have sometimes proved effective.

Conducting interviews

In one workshop, we conducted a mock interview in a humorous way. A reporter from the newspaper *Buscadrama* (Looking for Drama), interviewed a person who claimed to represent the Latino culture. The reporter asked the person questions about family relationships, conflict resolution and parenting techniques. After the fictitious character gave answers promoting patriarchy and violence, we asked the participants if they thought the character truly represented the Latino culture. We asked for their thoughts on alternative ways the culture could answer the same questions, and the participants created specific guidelines for promoting respect within the family.

In a similar way, in radio interviews we have conducted, we have played the roles of *Don Violento* (Mr Violence) and *Doña Respeto* (Ms Respect). Each character portrayed him or herself as a representative of the Latino culture. A dialogue ensued as a way of illustrating multiple cultural messages and inviting responsible choices. In these ways we explore the different depictions of Latino culture and their effects.

Through these processes and conversations many distinctions begin to be drawn: between the cultural practices the participants wish to identify with, and those they wish to challenge. We explore the construction of gender relations, with *el machismo* often identified as a significant factor in domestic violence.

'El Machismo' has deep roots. It is believed that if a woman is given respect in the home, the man is no longer a man. Other men call him sissy or say that he is tied to his wife's apron strings. (Olga)

The understanding of 'machismo' in the home goes from one generation to the next, like a tradition. (Noe)

In the process of these conversations, understandings of *'machismo'* are explored. These explorations open space for new understandings about Latino ways of being men and women, and invite participants to consider alternative Latino cultural messages that promote respectful relations.

One image that has been sold to us as part of our culture is 'machismo'. On the positive side is the idea of the 'macho' man who protects his family, nurtures respect and dignity. On the other side is the aberration, the antithesis, the negative use of power. (Raúl)

Although I observed abusive men when growing up, I think that one should respect women. I try not to do what I witnessed during my childhood. I am concerned about being a better father and person. There is a process of re-education for me. (Victor)

Creation of 'new' customs

As conversations are built around these themes of reclaiming respectful cultural traditions, at times there is a recognition that new customs, new ways of being are being created.

A new custom is beginning – women are supporting each other now. My mother did not have friends. The woman who had friends was considered a gossip. I have friends who advised me not to put up with so much violence in my home. I like the idea of having friends. When isolated, a woman can be convinced that violence is normal. I see different ways of living. (Lucía)

Articulating the liberatory elements within Latino culture makes these more available for participants to take up in their own lives. To aid this process we ask questions that invite a sense of agency in relation to how participants respond to the various cultural messages.

- *Given the same constellation of messages about domestic violence and the same general social environment, how is it that people organise their family relationships in different ways?*

- *What context is needed for people to step into preferred narratives?*

- *How can this context be created?*

- *What are the decisions and commitments that one has to make in order to reject violent practices?*

Often in these discussions not only is a sense of agency evoked but the meanings of committed action are explored. For example, it is regularly acknowledged that when participants take action to build upon respectful cultural messages, they honour both their ancestors and their children.

These explorations and acknowledgements lay the foundations for tracing the influence of the participants and the community on domestic violence. We seek to open space for participants to consider their own sense of agency in relation to domestic violence in their community. We have found that this type of questioning can help provide direction and movement in the workshops.

Tracing the influence of persons on problems

This stage of the workshop deals with rewriting narratives in the name of the Latino family. During this reconstruction phase, we ask questions that highlight unique or preferred outcomes: times when individuals, families or the community have stood *against* violence and *for* respectful relationships. The questions we ask seek to invite a sense of personal and community agency. As described by Michael White (1993), a sense of agency *is derived from the experience of escaping 'passengerhood' in life and from the sense of being able to play an active role in the shaping of one's own life* (p.59).

Through discussions and activities, we try to create a context in which participants can reconnect with knowledges, skills and ways of relating in their own lives that perhaps have been forgotten and that can become instruments for change. Participants begin to articulate times when they have already experienced pieces of solutions or engaged in behaviours useful to creating respectful relationships. These preferred outcomes are then woven into coherent narratives. Areas of strength and creativity come into focus.

> *I am from a family of independent women. I like to work outside the home. I think you can combine home life and work life. I can work part time and care for my home and child. My husband takes care of the baby too. He enjoys being with the baby. The two love each other very much.*
> (Patricia)

Participants begin to speak of their hopes and how they have held on to these dreams:

> *I have tried to work towards a home without violence. I have a vision of what it would be like. There wouldn't be bad words. The partners*

wouldn't throw things when they got mad. Everything would be more animated with more good humour and conversation about daily things. The partners would co-operate in order to share chores and money equally. (Lucía)

Significant relationships in the participants' lives which have fostered respect are honoured:

The person who inspired me was very respectful, very kind. He was interested in people and people respected him. There were certain things in his personality that I wanted to have. (Victor)

The ways in which people have got through hard times are explored:

Over the years I have come up with four things that have helped me reach my goals: common sense, honesty, optimism and, more than anything, a good sense of humour. These four things have helped me to survive and move forward. (Jorge)

Times in which people have made a stand against violent practices and the meanings of these actions are acknowledged:

It was a Thursday night. My wife and I were returning home after our last meeting in a series about domestic violence. For six months we had been attending these discussions. Returning home that night, my wife and I felt that a period of violence with its effects was ending. But something much more intense was waiting for us at home.

As we opened the door to the house, we were greeted by beautiful music, our eldest daughter bringing us flowers, our nine year old son bringing us a cake, and our youngest daughter handing us a card. The card said: 'Dad and Mom, We are very happy that today you are being reborn. We give you thanks for bringing new peace and respect into our home. We are proud of you'. And with tears and emotion that day, we understood that it was worth the effort to maintain a family without violence.

Three years have passed since that happened, and the memory of that night with our children continues to be the principal force that motivates us to maintain our family free of violence. (Guillermo)

The attributes that make up respectful relationships are also talked about:

Love is an art. As men we have to be prepared to see a woman as a companion with the same rights as men. If as parents we don't break the moulds then nothing will change. Children should be treated with respect. As men we must free ourselves of prejudices so that women cease to be subdued. (Victor)

Finding ways to authenticate these alternative narratives seems important. In some of our workshops, participants have used art supplies to create symbols representing lives dominated by violent practices and lives free from violent practices. Since the Latino culture is noted for symbolism, and since some of our participants cannot write, this exercise offers the opportunity for meaningful expression.

We have noticed that this is another stage of the workshop in which participants often respond *por el corazón* (through the heart). In our experience, participants tend to feel a renewed sense of resilience and hope as they focus on areas of strength and creativity in their lives, and on the histories that support their attempts at change. We ask a specific question that builds on this heart-felt response and serves as an impetus for change: 'What most motivates you to stand *against* violent acts and *for* respectful relationships?' Participants almost unanimously reply: *Our love for our families and our children.* Time after time, they state that this love is what will sustain them during the difficult process of making changes toward homes without violence.

On the basis of this dedication to family and to a future without violence, we move into the next segment of the workshop.

Translating narratives into concrete actions

During our workshops, participants have consistently expressed their desire to deal with the concrete matters involved in domestic violence. They have requested information on community resources and have asked for time in the workshops when participants could share suggestions and advice. In response to this feedback, we spend time with participants exploring practical steps that can be taken into their lives to promote more respectful relationships. Participants often speak about how they feel a sense of empowerment in being able to leave the workshops with concrete steps that they can take immediately. Information is given on local resources and support groups that specialise in the prevention and remediation of domestic violence. For different community members different steps will be appropriate. Some women may want to approach other women or women's organisations for support, some men may feel the need to join groups to address their violence. Some participants are motivated to join parenting classes or leadership trainings offered by a local multicultural program and created by members of the Latino community.

Community ideas to prevent and transform violence

Other practical steps may be of a different nature. Within the workshop a number of guidelines are often proposed by the community for those participants who wish to cease perpetrating domestic violence. We wish to honour the contributions of all the participants without in any way diminishing the effects of violence, or participating in the mystification of responsibility for violence. We work with the suggestions given by the community in ways that invite those perpetrating violence to take responsibility for this violence. Here is an example of a list of guidelines proposed by participants in the workshops.

- Tell yourself that there are non-violent alternatives to expressing anger and frustration.
- Realise that hitting doesn't help.
- Communicate when there is a problem.
- Express yourself peacefully and explain your feelings: *Members of a family have to talk and come to agreements.* (Ana)
- Ask for things with respect.
- Respect the personal space and possessions of others.
- Remember that in order to receive you must give.
- Dialogue with your partner about the stress of racism and economic problems: come to mutual decisions about how to deal with these problems.

- Wait for drunkenness to pass before talking.
- Ask for help with parenting and get together with other parents.
- Be a good parent by giving good advice and examples to the children: *Parents have to teach their children all that they know. The first schooling takes place at home.* (Ana)
- Avoid competition between parents to win your children's love.
- Take responsibility for what you do in the home because it is very possible that the children will repeat what you do when they are adults.
- Take a walk, leave the situation mentally or physically in order to see things differently.
- Recognise your violent actions and ask for help.
- Think about the beautiful aspects of the culture – celebrations and customs that demonstrate respect among people.

These suggestions offered by the community can become steps in a long journey toward more respectful family relationships. What seems significant is that these proposals are derived from a collective community response appropriate to Latino ways. We believe that this process offers a profound invitation from the community to those who have perpetrated violence. It is an invitation for individuals to play their part within a context of broader collective action. Although this step is close to the end of our workshop, it represents in reality the beginning of new processes. It is as if the seeds of respect have been sown and now the process of care and nourishment must continue. As Raúl describes, this is a community responsibility:

People are becoming more aware of the theme of domestic violence and talking about it more. No longer is it an exclusively private topic but instead a community concern.

Closing ceremony

At the end of the workshop, Latin American music is played to enhance the sense of solidarity among the participants and the connection with cultural roots. We join with participants to form a circle. One member of our team reviews what has taken place during the workshop. Each participant is asked to share something learned during the workshop and a potential next step in his or her preferred direction. This public commitment promotes a strengthening of newly formed ideas and decisions within a culturally comfortable environment.

A member of the team then reminds participants of the corn plant as a metaphor for the family. As toxins can interrupt the life cycle of the corn plant, so violent practices can interrupt the development of respectful family relationships. And, just as with the corn plant, continued nourishment can make it possible for the Latino family to grow to benefit the Latino community and the world as a whole. Despite the fact that the workshop deals with a difficult subject, we have found that it invariably ends in a spirit of unity. We believe that this is a catalyst for future change. Participants and facilitators express appreciation for the mutual sharing. We leave with new approaches for our challenges and renewed hope for the future.

Note

This paper is an extract from a longer article that was published in the *Dulwich Centre Newsletter,* 1998 No.1. Republished here with permission.

The authors can be contacted via email at: Jesús Tovar: Gamba7@aol.com; Pamela Montgomery: Pamela408@aol.com; Alberto Colorado: chulel2000@yahoo.com

References

Jenkins, A. 1990: *Invitations to Responsibility: The therapeutic engagement of men who are violent and abusive.* Adelaide: Dulwich Centre Publications.

White, M. 1993: 'Deconstruction and therapy.' In Gilligan, S. & Price, R. (eds), *Therapeutic Conversations,* pp.22-61. New York: WWNorton & Co.

White, M. & Epston, D. 1990: *Narrative Means to Therapeutic Ends.* New York: WWNorton & Co.

9.

Lesbians and bisexual women working together against violence

The story of Bradley-Angle House

adapted from a paper by

Beth Crane, Jeannie La France, Gillian Leightling,
Brooks Nelson & Erika Silver[1]

We were not mom and apple pie in any sense of the word. A few of us were mothers, but we were prostitutes. We were lesbians. We were drug addicts. We were alcoholics. We were considered the scum of society who had brought this on ourselves and deserved whatever shit we were living through. (Bonnie[2])

Bradley-Angle House is a feminist social change domestic violence intervention agency in Portland, Oregon. We began in 1971 as 'Prescott House' primarily as a shelter for women who were coming out of prison, and also women who were prostituted and/or in the gay bar scene. Many of the women who started the house were working-class lesbian/dyke feminists who had been to prison and were involved with the street community.

In 1975 the shelter was renamed in memory of two women – Sharon Bradley and Pam Angle – whose lives included a lot of violence and who had died, and the focus shifted towards support for women escaping violence in intimate relationships. The founders chose this direction because there were no services for women leaving domestic violence, and there were high number of requests for help from battered women and their children.

The agency started very informally and gradually built up from the grassroots. We have grown to a staff of eighteen. We provide a twenty-four-hour hotline, shelter, children's program, support groups, transitional services, community education, and technical assistance on family violence issues. Most of our work goes into responding to the effects of men's violence. Over time we have also developed specific services to provide to lesbians, bisexual women, and other members of sexual minority communities. This paper focuses solely on the work of the Lesbian and Bisexual Caucuses of Bradley-Angle House and the services which they have developed.

Services for women who have experienced the violence of other women

In 1986 one of the shelter staff, a lesbian, was approached by another lesbian woman about battering in her lesbian relationship and asked if she could stay at the shelter. Even though shelter staff had been through anti-homophobia training, there was a lot of denial about lesbian battering. The woman came to the shelter and struggled with whether or not to be out. This was the impetus for some lesbian and non-lesbian staff to begin serious discussion about how to address lesbian battering more effectively. It was decided that we'd establish a support group run for and by lesbians.

Advertisements were taken out in local queer papers and flyers were posted throughout the community. Calls were slow to come in at first but, once it began, the group flourished and has now been going continually for over ten years. Workers from the group have spoken at conferences, developed brochures, and facilitated community forums on issues such as: what is abuse, and how do oppression and abuse interact and affect relationships?

Practical considerations

In trying to respond appropriately to lesbian and bisexual women in relation to their experiences of violence, there have been various practical considerations that we have had to take into account. Our current practice is to ask women when they first call about groups – how they identify: lesbian, bi, or heterosexual. They are then referred to the appropriate intake worker.

The intakes to the group for women who have experienced the violence of other women are more involved than for the general domestic violence support groups. Trying to get beyond a snapshot view of relationships, we need to get information about the context of the relationship as a whole. We only have the perspective of the woman we are talking to; however, the more information we have the better. We use a check-list to have a better understanding of who did what: who started it; who escalated it; if there was self-defence, what did it look like. We need to get this kind of information to keep the women in the group safe. This can be a difficult issue. The reality is that, unlike heterosexual battering, without care being taken the perpetrator can potentially access services.

Anti-oppression work

Anti-oppression work with staff and volunteers is one of the most important steps that domestic violence shelters can take to better serve lesbian and bi-women survivors, as well as make their programs more accessible and safer for all women.

In 1991-1992 shelter staff wanted to better support lesbian survivors and provide anti-homophobia education with the shelter residents. We reviewed our phone screening process, shelter intake, children's intake, and shelter rules. We identified thirty to forty shelter programs to request shelter rules and materials, drawing from rural/urban areas and geographic areas with higher concentrations of communities of colour. We researched our archives for original shelter rules. We found some materials from the earliest days requesting women to find another space to 'make love in'.

We developed a revised phone screening process which included asking: 'How do you feel about living with women from different races, class, religion; or women who may be lesbian or bisexual?' We had already been screening for racism and communal living issues, however, adding the words lesbian and bisexual has a number of effects: (1) it lets lesbian and bisexual callers know that we take their physical and emotional safety seriously, and that we are advocates for lesbians and bisexuals, (2) it lets straight women know our expectations about respect, communication, and community living issues, and (3) it lets battered heterosexual women know that it is safe for them to re-evaluate their sexuality as an effect of domestic violence in their lives.

We wanted women to feel safe enough to bring out their general feelings, thoughts and questions. Our phone screening process helps us gently identify homophobia as misinformation or stereotypes. At the time we were the only shelter in the state actively screening all callers for homophobia and compatibility with diversity. Callers are not expected to have perfect responses, and they do not. When issues of oppression, whether racism, classism or homophobia, come up, staff and volunteers respectfully 'probe' for a willingness to consider accurate information, self-reflection, and personal growth. We are clear about the profoundly unhelpful effects of stereotypes about battered women, and this often creates the possibility for changes in perception about other stereotypes.

At around the same time, shelter rules were amended to clarify respect for diversity. Statements which are derogatory towards people of colour, welfare recipients, lesbians, or others, can now be grounds enough to ask someone to leave. By clearly communicating the shelter's expectations ahead of time, we encourage participants to ask for help to re-evaluate stereotypes or misinformation. One of two weekly house meetings focus on issues of oppression and their connection to sexism and domestic violence.

In addition to offering shelter to battered lesbians, bisexuals and their children, we also offer an option to provide a motel voucher for women who have confidentiality issues connected to domestic violence movement staff and volunteers, the lesbian community, or concerns about homophobic targeting by other residents. Motel vouchers are also an alternative for providing shelter to women who identify as trans. Bradley-Angle is still working on developing policies around trans issues. Our most recent step has been to establish a policy which states, 'All our services are open to persons who identify as women regardless of their participation in medically-based transition'. We realise, however, that we still have a long way to go to make trans women feel comfortable using our services.

Volunteer training

In our volunteer training, much time is devoted to unlearning different oppressions. The anti-homophobia training is divided for the majority of the training with straight women and 'queer' women working separately. Each group is facilitated in pairs with at least one lesbian or bi-woman. Lesbian and bisexual women focus on unlearning internalised oppression. Heterosexual women get a general unlearning homophobia training as well as specific tools for shelter and crisis phone work. Something as simple as not assigning a gender to the batterer until the caller does, makes the program more accessible to sexual minority women. Imagine the impact on a survivor who calls a crisis line because she can't believe what is happening to her, and the advocate gives her the message that it is not really happening because all batterers are male.

Bisexual women

In July 1991 a bisexual woman went through the Bradley-Angle volunteer training. At the time, the anti-homophobia training was being divided into lesbian and straight women so that the different issues of unlearning homophobia and internalised homophobia could be dealt with in a safe environment. The volunteer raised her hand and asked, 'Where do the bisexuals go?' The facilitator said, 'That's never come up before, I'll leave that up to you'. This was indicative of much of the early work that Bradley-Angle did on same-sex issues. Bisexual women were invisible.

The history of bisexual women at Bradley-Angle is difficult to track. Because of this bisexual volunteer's experience, we believe that there had been other bi women in training for several years. Those women chose to join either the straight or lesbian group as they were the only two options offered. Many bi women probably chose to identify either with the lesbian or straight community in other parts of the agency.

The volunteer co-ordinator was responsive and suggested a separate group for the bi women. This didn't work, however, because of the complexities of sexual identity. Since then, the sexual minority groups have remained together and have brainstormed stereotypes of lesbians and bisexuals, as well as talking about other issues of internalised bi and homophobia. Discussion also includes the relationships between the lesbian and bi women's communities. Lesbian and bi women co-facilitate this training together.

Around the same time, another bisexual woman was hired as Outreach Co-ordinator. She expressed interest in either forming a joint lesbian/bi women's caucus or joining the work group on lesbian battering. The lesbian caucus decided to remain lesbian only. The work group on lesbian battering vacillated in regard to the issue. At one point the work group invited bisexual participation on a project and then decided against it later on. It was suggested that the (two out) bi women form their own caucus. Despite a rocky beginning, the caucus gained members slowly but surely. Soon bi women from other domestic and sexual violence programs started attending. The group is both social/support and task oriented. The group has spent a lot of time problem-solving issues of biphobia within the battered women's movement, and issues that battered bisexual women face.

These discussions were often difficult. Many problems have been resolved; however, it is important to chronicle the homophobia and biphobia that bi women experience in order to improve services and work in coalition with lesbians. For example, bisexual women often identify specific events or beliefs on the part of the lesbian community as biphobic. The lesbian community perceives this as homophobia on the part of the bi women's community. Both communities respond similarly to each other's reactions, and a cycle is born. Bi women wanted the lesbian support group to be open to bi women battered by women. Lesbians on the staff felt that it was important to deal with same-sex domestic violence in a lesbian-only space. Thus, bi women feel excluded and lesbians feel disrespected. Each group feels like the other group's sentiments come from an oppressive place.

During bi caucus discussions, members tried to be aware of the dynamics of the intersections of internalised homophobia, straight privilege, and external biphobia. Many issues centred around specific barriers to bi women in same-sex domestic violence relationships, including: lack of appropriate services to bi women battered by women; disagreement about how these services should be provided; a sense from the lesbian community that it was unethical or even abusive to be a bi woman and in a relationship with a lesbian; exclusion of or not acknowledging the work of bi women on same-sex domestic violence. One supervisor attempted to obstruct the beginning of the bi women's caucus. In this atmosphere, it was acceptable to make assumptions and generalisations about bisexuals and their behaviour. Comments were made about how bisexuality did not exist or was perverted, or that the bisexual's organising was disrespectful to lesbians.

Many issues faced by bi women survivors of same-sex domestic violence are similar to those faced by lesbians, for example, perpetrators (whether they are lesbian or bi) may use the accusations of 'not being a real lesbian', or not being 'really committed to a relationship', or 'too much under the power of men', to shame bisexuals into staying in the relationship longer. Issues that may be different include bi women staying in abusive relationships to prove that bisexuals do not leave women for men, or to disprove the stereotype that bisexuals cannot last in any relationship. Abusers use threats of outing the woman to the straight or lesbian community. Jealousy and scrutiny of behaviour is compounded when the batterer accuses the survivor of being 'twice as likely to mess around on them'. Bisexuals are also further isolated because the community is small and not cohesive.

Many of these initial conflicts and oppressive behaviours have greatly improved over time. The group for battered lesbians is now a woman-to-woman domestic violence group open to lesbians, bi women and women who do not identify as either. We have also held the first ever workshops on bisexuality and domestic violence in this area, and continue to work to change the language in Bradley-Angle to be inclusive of bisexuals.

Lesbians and Bisexuals in Alliance (LABIA)

Over time, individuals from both the bi caucus and lesbian caucus took leadership in bringing both groups together. This important process included belief on the part of both caucuses in the goodness of the other. It was helpful that there was also a lot of mutual respect and friendship as this helped bridge the hurt feelings and disagreements that occurred at times. Throughout, we had the mutual goals of providing respectful services to women battered by women and the vision of an ever-strengthening movement. Some ways we have built coalition between lesbians and bi women have included: joint work projects with equal lesbian and bi women participation, a joint lesbian and bi women's caucus that meets quarterly, and social time together. The lesbian and bi caucuses work together now to organise our community forums about same-sex domestic violence. Lesbians and bisexuals support each other while resisting becoming invisible in our work together. Recently we held a series of forums focusing on accountability and appropriate community response to lesbian battering. We also do person-to-person outreach, training of other organisations' staff and volunteers, outreach to bartenders at women's bars, and outreach to other services within the community.

Closing

This paper would not have been possible without the dedication of the lesbian, bisexual and straight women who have committed themselves to providing the highest quality of service and support to other women who are the survivors of violence. All women have the right to live with dignity and respect, and without violence. Many lesbians and bisexual women have taken risks, and provided brilliant analyses which contribute to our work today. These women continue to influence our future directions.

We remember.

Notes

This paper was originally published in the special issue of the *Dulwich Centre Journal* entitled: 'Bisexuality: Identity, politics and partnerships' (1999 No.1).

1. The authors can be contacted c/o Jeannie LaFrance, email: actforaction@hotmail Or write to Bradley-Angle House, PO Box 14694, Portland, OR 97293, USA.

2. This quote comes from the book *The Women of Bradley-Angle House* (1978) self-published by the women of Bradley-Angle House, Portland, Oregon.

10.

Working with young men

Taking a stand

against sexual abuse and

sexual harassment

by

Ginny Slattery[1]

The Adolescent Sexual Abuse Prevention Program (Mary Street) within which I work, engages with young people aged between 12-18 who have committed a sexual offence, or who have engaged in inappropriate or offensive sexual behaviour, or sexual harassment. Mary Street provides counselling and help for adolescents and their families or caregivers. We aim to assist young people to:

- take responsibility to stop sexual abuse and sexual harassment,
- make restitution to help heal the harm caused by sexual abuse and sexual harassment,
- respect others and develop appropriate relationships,
- build self-respect and confidence,
- find ways of making sexuality respectful and positive.

The program works co-operatively with police, courts, welfare agencies and schools to achieve outcomes that put priority on the safety and well-being of younger children and those at risk, and which are fair for all people concerned.

The therapeutic framework used in the program is primarily based on an invitational approach that utilises processes of respectful engagement, accountability and restitution. The framework stems from the innovative work done by Rob Hall (1996) and Alan Jenkins (1998) with male perpetrators of violence and sexual abuse.

The framework at Mary Street, however, is very much 'work in progress' as Alan, Rob and I continue to be influenced by work happening in other programs, by the ongoing contributions of men and women working in this area, and by the victims and their families.

My experience of this work

Most of my management and clinical experience as a family therapist has been in the area of violence and abuse, particularly family preservation work. Consequently, I have some understanding of the struggles experienced by those of us who work in this exciting but very challenging area. When I first joined the Mary Street program, however, I was unprepared for some of the feelings that started to creep up on me during those early months.

It is hard to put those feelings into words. It was like a heaviness started to creep into my life. I noticed that although I still could connect with lightness, happiness, and a positive outlook, my life was developing an overcast quality. This heaviness was like a greyness or cloudiness that just hung around me like a shadow.

Over time, I worked out that this heaviness and these grey clouds were made up of a mixture of different sorts of thoughts and feelings, particularly sadness and anger. I experienced sadness about the empty and sometimes alienated space the young men I was working with inhabited; sadness about how much hurt they had caused in the lives of others; and anger and outrage at what they had put others through.

I also experienced confusion. The young men who sat in front of me in the counselling room seemed incapable of such selfishness. I would experience disbelief and the feelings that accompany loss of hope and loss of faith. I also experienced fear that I may be making inappropriate judgements and that the young men would re-offend.

At times I noticed myself preoccupied with thinking about what the young man had done. I would sometimes experience intrusive imagery involving acts of abuse. One of the most startling effects on me of this heaviness, however, was a sense of disconnection from those around me.

It is not as if I find it difficult to understand the prevalence of abuse. When I consider that the dominant blueprints in society for men, women and relationships have been shaped by narratives promoting hierarchy, patriarchy and the assignment of roles and self-worth to individuals based on gender, class, race, sexuality, economic status, and control of self and others, it makes more sense to me that in this context, all kinds of abuse can flourish. It makes sense to me that these narratives have many negative outcomes for the emotional life of individuals and communities.

It was also not as if this was the first time I had struggled with some of these feelings. But this was a different kind of heaviness, one with which I was not familiar. On reflection, I think this was due to a combination of the following factors: firstly, knowing the details of the offences; secondly, working with one client group all the time (in other jobs I have always had a range of clients); and thirdly, I think it is connected to being a woman doing this work.

Doing this work brings me, on a daily basis, close to certain gendered ideas and practices, for example, the sexualised objectification of women, the extraordinary sense of entitlement that some young men can have when it comes to exploring their sexual interests, and the gendered justifications for taking advantage of others' vulnerabilities as a response to one's own feelings of powerlessness. Being a woman, I am a member of a group that stands to suffer the terrible consequences of these attitudes and ways of thinking. I am conscious that in some circumstances they can also have terrible consequences for men and male children.

The trap of totalising ideas

In trying to understand the heaviness that I described above, I realised that at times in my work I was becoming trapped in judgements, and stuck in suspiciousness or mistrust with my clients. I was at times coming to totalising and oppressive views of them. I discovered myself being particularly vulnerable to negative, reductionist narratives about men and masculinity. I believe that there is a place for a healthy, critical scepticism in this work. However, this can so easily turn into an unhealthy mistrust.

Although I have always been informed by feminist and gender analyses of men's ways of being, and I am committed to bringing this political framework to therapy, I started to recognise that the emotional effects of the work – the heaviness – could make me blind at times to genuinely listening and acknowledging times of difference and the diversity in these young men's lived experience. I noticed that I was vulnerable to letting some of the ideas and knowledge I have about patriarchy, and its implications for masculinity, shape my work with clients, rather than allowing my work with clients to shape my ideas.

I have noticed that when I am in the grip of heaviness and greyness, it is much harder for me to hear and notice the moments of resistance to patriarchy in these young men's lives, and to really explore in a thorough way the diversity of their lived experience. Another way of saying this is that it becomes harder for me to privilege hope above despair, and easier to resort to totalising views of these young men.

I realised that if I didn't find a way around the heaviness, I would be at risk of not upholding my commitment and responsibility to genuine curiosity and collaboration in my work with young men. This position requires, on my part, a capacity to draw on socio-political analyses in my observations and conversations with young men, but not to impose these analyses.

I knew that there must be a way around this heaviness that would take into account the reality of the sexual offences committed by the young men, but that wouldn't trap me in totalising views of men and masculinity or get me to give up on one of my core beliefs: that human life is too diverse and complex to be comprehended through uni-dimensional lenses.

One of the reasons I knew that there must be ways through this dilemma was that I have always had, and continue to have, equitable and wonderfully close and supportive relationships with men in all aspects of my life. Whilst these relationships have some gendered aspects to them (because they have developed in a social context that has historically promoted certain roles for people along the lines of gender and power), there are many aspects of these relationships that stand outside of or go beyond gendered prescriptions. Positive and equal relationships are rich in their diversity and creativity. While in no way diminishing the power and effects of gender relations on men and women's lives, it is my own experience that the creative process of life and relationships can be more powerful than the restraints of negative social role stereotyping and dominant discourse.

So, this job really invited me as a woman to re-examine, in an honest way, my position on gender and masculinity. It invited me to consider a position that is genuinely collaborative and accountable to the young men I work with, and that does not totalise masculinity.

The rest of this article will explore ways of thinking about masculinity, and working with young men who sexually offend, that help to guard against the effects of those 'grey clouds' diminishing both my own life and the quality of my work.

I will firstly present some experiences in my clinical work that have shaped how I think about masculinity. Secondly, I will articulate some key notions and assumptions about identity and masculinity that I draw upon to guard against totalising practices. And lastly, I will articulate some practice principles I am developing to assist me, as a woman, in this project, and some examples from my clinical work that reflect how these ideas can be translated into a process and a language that connects with young men.

Acknowledging the struggle reflected by young men's lived experience

There is a commitment in our program to assist young men to name unhelpful ideas they hold which promote sexually abusive actions. To facilitate this process with them, we will often deconstruct some of the dominant stories about men and masculinity that circulate in white, western culture. When I listen to the meanings that young men ascribe to their sexually abusive actions and the dilemmas they face as they attempt to honour their commitment to stop abuse, it is apparent to me that they are often engaged in a genuine struggle. This struggle, in my view, is the outcome of their identity being entangled within the ideas of dominant masculinity, but at the same time questioning whether to believe them or not.

Although the young men in the program may have ceased the sexually abusive behaviour for which they were referred to the program, it is not uncommon for them to still be engaged in other abusive practices. These practices may include minor sexual harassment, resorting to violence to resolve conflict, and 'talking dirty' about women when in the company of other young men. Although they may have stopped sexually abusing younger children, they may still be resorting to coercive and manipulative practices to express their sexual or romantic interest in young women of their own age.

The fact that these young men have stopped some abusive actions but are still practising others, suggests that they are questioning, to some extent, the validity of dominant masculine ideals and their implications for identity. As I get closer to understanding this struggle that young men are having about whether or not to engage in certain ideas, it is evident to me that their relationship with identity and masculinity constitutes a vital part of this struggle.

I believe that for young men to come to terms with their sexual offences, to take charge of this struggle, and to make a genuine lifelong commitment to respectful sexuality and ways of relating, it is not enough for them to address their sexually abusive actions and engage in some form of restitution. It is also necessary for them to address, in a comprehensive way, their relationship with masculinity and, in particular, their relationship with some oppressive ideas or attitudes that underlay a construction of masculinity that promotes abusive behaviour.

Therefore, in my work with many of my clients, I am finding it increasingly helpful to construct two particular projects. Firstly, the project of addressing their sexually abusive actions, and secondly, the project of addressing their relationship with masculinity. It is my opinion that these two projects are not separate, but in reality are intricately interrelated. For my clients, however, situating their sexually abusive actions within this broader context of their relationship with masculinity is not always straightforward. Most young men would never have engaged in a conversation about gendered aspects of identity before coming to Mary Street. One way that I have found helpful to begin these conversations is by using externalising conversations – about masculinity, about the unhelpful ideas that contribute to abusive actions, and about the young men's relationship with masculinity which is often constructed as a journey.

This orientation to our conversations allows me to relate with these young men as people who have a relationship with masculinity which influences their identity, rather than as young men who are products of dominant masculinity, and whose actions are primarily determined by patriarchal values.

It also enables me to notice and engage with these young men's other ways of being and actions that don't fit within dominant conceptions of masculinity. I am able to externalise and explore the struggle that is reflected by the contradictions in these young men's lived experience. This relational framework helps me to avoid totalising views of the young men with whom I work, and to step into an understanding of their struggle. This is a struggle that exists because of these young men's interest in and engagement with alternative values. This orientation also broadens out the process of therapeutic inquiry to include explorations of the wider political journey that young men take in the process of constructing their masculine identity.

Key notions and assumptions about masculinity which influence my clinical work

The notion of there being a relationship between young men's identity and masculinity is fraught with difficulty because both these terms have a range of meanings and associated practices in different contexts. Some of the key assumptions and ways of thinking that I draw upon in my clinical work are those which assist me to put into practice this relational way of thinking about masculinity. These ways of thinking are also congruent with my own personal values and experience. Here I have listed some of the key assumptions about masculinity that guide my work:

- Masculinity has multiple and contradictory meanings and different significance in different social contexts (Hare-Mustin 1996).

- Dominant constructions of masculinity for young men are informed by patriarchal ideas and values. Some of these ideas and values have significant negative outcomes.[2] These negative aspects of masculinity promoted by patriarchy create a context for the problematic behaviours we deal with at Mary Street – sexual harassment and sexual abuse

- Masculinity for young men is also informed by the political and social context in contemporary society, and this includes social/cultural movements in contemporary society. Feminism and ideas about equality influence to some extent the ways in which young men construct their identities. Perhaps most significant in this regard are the programs in mainstream media and schooling that acknowledge the relationship between gender and socialisation. The young men I work with often demonstrate an awareness and understanding of feminist ideals and those values upheld by pro-diversity movements, despite experiencing contradictions between the ideas represented by these social changes and their own lived experience.

- Therefore, contemporary masculinity for young men is informed by competing sets of ideas and discourses rather than a single set of values promoted in patriarchy.

Key notions and assumptions about identity which influence my clinical work

There are a number of key ways of thinking about identity that inform my work. I have listed a number of these here.

- Identity is not the result of a fixed personality or the unfolding of a true nature but results from the active participation in a process of interpretation and construction of experience (see White 1996).

- Identity is relational. Identity is constructed through sets of relationships and associated ideas, not just through our relationships with people but also through our relationships with ideas (see Bird 1999; Freedman & Combs 1999). (For further perspectives on relational frameworks, refer to the recent publication by Johnella Bird [2000].)

- The relationship between identity and masculinity is something that can change and be renegotiated.

- Each young man's relationship with masculinity is unique.

- Adolescence is a time when young people are already preoccupied with a personal journey in which they are committed to identity exploration and formation, and emerging sexuality constitutes a significant part of this journey.

In summary, the above-mentioned ways of thinking about masculinity and identity assist me to avoid totalising practices in my work with young men. They enable me to develop a context for researching parts of their lives that reflect a commitment and interest in values which honour respect and responsibility.

Linking these ideas to practice: six practice principles

The final section of this paper will outline six practice principles, stemming from the above-mentioned ways of thinking about masculinity and identity, that I find helpful in assisting young men to address their relationship with masculinity, and in assisting me to step into an appreciation of the complexity of their lived experience.

1. Practice principle one: Listening for openings

This practice involves listening for:

- Clues about what constitutes this young man's unique relationship with masculinity.

- Evidence of some sort of struggle between competing/opposing masculinities.

An example: John's story

John had been attending the Mary Street program for a few months to address his charge of indecent assault against a seven-year-old girl. An example of *listening for openings* emerged when I noticed a pattern developing in my conversations with John. At the beginning of counselling sessions with John, I would often ask him about any effects that the last session had had on him, and what sort of thoughts had gone through his mind about some of the things we had talked about. John would pretty much always respond with: 'Nothing, I didn't think about it. After I leave here I just forget about it.'

I could understand this response to a certain extent, however, I started to feel unnerved by it and also concerned. John had done some really good work in acknowledging and facing his sexually abusive behaviour and, as far as I could be sure, had stuck to his commitment not to sexually offend again. I wondered, however, how I could invite this young man to reflect on his relationship with masculinity outside the therapy room – for without this I feared that all his good work could become undone.

I decided to ask John about this. After I commented on this pattern, I asked him what he thought this forgetting was about. John did not say much at first and then replied: 'I'm a different person when I come here. It is like I am made up of all different kinds of people. There are all different sides to me. I am a different person in different parts of my life. If you saw me on the street with my friends, you would not recognise me.'

I became very curious about this and I had a hunch that this compartmentalisation was possibly speaking about John's relationship with masculinity. I decided to identify this compartmentalisation as an *opening* which contained clues about John's unique relationship with masculinity. It also seemed to constitute evidence of a struggle that John was having about juggling competing masculinities. I began to ask him lots of questions about the different people in different parts of his life, what sorts of values they stood for and what they did. This process led to a discovery that in some contexts of John's life he was being pushed around by some ideas about toughness. These ideas about toughness could wield considerable influence for two reasons: firstly, because the degrees to which he displayed toughness influenced the degree of respect he would gain from other men; and secondly, toughness seemed very important in order to protect himself from other men. In these conversations, John also explained his indecent assault of the young girl in terms of it being an act of revenge – that he had needed to 'prove a point by hurting someone else' in the way he had been hurt.

We took a lot of time to explore these experiences and understandings, and it became apparent to me that John's relationship with masculinity was dominated by a kind of compartmentalisation and struggle that occurs when the different domains of one's life are sustained by different sets of values.

At one point during this therapeutic process, I asked John *which of these people he steps into fit the most with 'who he is'*. John listed the domains of his life where he is not 'different people' but is 'himself'. I was relieved to hear that Mary Street was one of these domains. This suggested to me that the ways in which John was relating during our sessions together was congruent with the preferred values and ideas that he held about his life and identity.

Another question I asked John during this time was: *That is really interesting. I am not sure about those other people or sides, who they are, what they do, but what would your life look like if you were to take this person you are at Mary Street into all other parts of your life rather than leaving him behind?*

Over time I was able to invite a commitment from John to challenge this compartmentalisation as it became evident that most of the trouble that was happening in his life occurred in the domains of his life where Mr Tough Guy and Mr Bully lived. These identities would get him proving his point in dangerous ways and in ways that would take advantage of younger people in vulnerable circumstances. Together, we were then able to embark on a second project that involved John addressing his relationship with masculinity. This new project ran alongside his work in addressing the particular indecent assault charge that had brought him to Mary Street.

Another example: Andrew's story

An *opening* became available to me in my conversations with Andrew when he described *the events that led up to his offending behaviour.* This young man was referred to the program after being charged with indecent assault and indecent exposure. He had followed a woman closely, grabbed her and then exposed himself to her. The events that led up to him committing this offence constituted a struggle he was having as to whether or not to join a male gang, and being told that to be a member of this gang he would have to engage in this act. I became curious as to why such an act would secure membership in this gang, and what membership in a gang would mean for him. I had a sense that these issues were connected to his relationship with masculinity.

When I asked him more about what led him to decide to engage in this act, he talked about proving that he can be tough and cool by picking on others without caring about it – *a relationship with masculinity that is dominated by proving a point in dangerous ways.*

Some of the questions I asked Andrew during this time included:

How would membership in this gang benefit you?

What do you think you were setting out to prove to yourself, to the others?
What do you think of this idea, that it is tough to pick on others without caring about it?

Do you think other young men get tricked by this idea?

Andrew and I were then able to construct a project that would involve addressing 'proving it' and would explore his abusive practices in the wider context of the unhelpful ideas that are promoted by various dominant constructions of masculinity.

2. **Practice principle two: Exploring and documenting the young man's unique relationship with masculinity**

Once an *opening* in therapy has revealed some information about what constitutes the young man's unique relationship with masculinity, the following processes can be utilised:

- Explore all domains of their life in which this relationship is actualised; e.g. school, sport activities, personal relationships, etc.

- Explore the effects of this relationship on others and on his understandings of his own identity.

- Name and deconstruct behaviours he is engaged in, either willingly or unwillingly, to prove negative constructions of masculinity.

- Listen for times of difference in these domains when the young man is not resorting to behaviours shaped by dominant notions of masculinity. These times reflect a questioning of these ideas and evidence of a struggle with them.

I have listed here some examples of questions that I have found can assist in exploring and documenting the young person's unique relationship with masculinity:

What is it like to find yourself in situations where you feel expected to go along with ideas that you don't like or don't personally agree with?

What is it like, do you think, for women/men to be around men who always go along with these ideas?

Are there times when you don't get bossed around by these ideas?

What sort of values do these times fit with?

Which voice do these values fit with? The voice of toughness or your own voice?

If you were to be true to your own voice more, what would happen to your relationship with manhood? Would it work better for you? Would you start to have this relationship more on your own terms rather than on the terms of toughness?

3. **Practice principle three: Exploring a commitment and interest from the young man to address the aspects of his relationship with masculinity that have negative implications for himself and others**

Once we have explored together the meaning and experience of the young man's unique relationship with masculinity, I have found it helpful to explicitly invite the young man to make a commitment to address the aspects of this relationship that are having problematic effects.

The sorts of questions that can create space for an articulation of such a commitment include:

Do you want to find ways to address this conflict/struggle that is going on for you?

What will it mean if you don't find a way through this?

What would it mean to the child/person you hurt if you don't address these things?

If you did work on this job in a serious way, would you be more likely or less likely to get into sexually harassing, sexually abusive actions again?

What would your local community be like if other young men having a similar struggle were to take your lead in facing these issues?

An important aspect of this inquiry involves finding out about some of the consequences that young men will face as they take a stand against some of the dominant expectations of masculinity. This is important because it may involve their own lives being threatened by other young men. The negative effects on young men of making decisions to stand against some negative constructions of masculinity cannot be underestimated. Many of the young men I see describe themselves as being continuously on guard and in a state of fear, as they strive to firstly gain respect from their male peers, and also to protect themselves from the aggression that sustains some relationships between young men. There can be a lot at stake when young men endeavour to prove themselves and stand up for themselves without resorting to violence and sexism. As a therapist, I feel a sense of responsibility to understand the complexities of young men's lives and to step into a supportive role with them as we explore together in counselling, safe ways of negotiating their way through these dilemmas.

4. Practice principle four: Setting up review mechanisms and accountability structures

This practice principle involves setting up review mechanisms and accountability structures whereby those affected by the young man's relationship with masculinity are consulted as he endeavours to take up different practices and ways of being.

An example of such an accountability structure is reflected by a process that my colleague, Rob Hall, and I set up for a young man who was living in a residential facility whilst attending the program. During our therapy with this young person, it became evident that he had some ways of relating with women staff at the unit that did not fit with the commitments he was making at Mary Street to honour respect and responsibility in relationships.

Once we had assisted the young man to identify that this was something he wanted to address, we suggested to him that Rob or I contact the unit occasionally to consult with the women staff about how they were experiencing his attempts to relate in alternative respectful ways with them. When the young man agreed to this idea, the women staff were then able to build on the young man's success in this project, and contribute in a positive way to his work at Mary Street.

5. Practice principle five: Connecting with young people's energy and honouring their culture

As an adult worker having conversations with young people, there are certain orientations to my work that I feel are important. These include acknowledging and utilising the enthusiasm and excitement of young people as a resource.

Adolescence is a time in which identity is being formed not only in relationship to other people but also the broader world. Young people are seeking a way in which they can take their place in the broader community and are trying to create identities through which to do so.

In this work, I have found it helpful to link young men's personal struggles with their broader political implications. These are conversations that young men seem very interested in as they involve considerations about the contributions they can make to their community.

Here are some examples of questions that can link the personal with the political, and that explore the contributions young men may wish to make to the broader community:

Do you want to have a place in creating a different kind of society or will you be content to just watch it go by?

If you were to not just talk about this project but also live it and redesign some of your relationship with manhood on your own terms, what will it mean for the next generation of young men and women?

When you come to the end of your life, years and years from now, do you want to be able to look back and see that you did more than just follow the crowd? That you made this world a better place, a fairer place for both men and women?

Will sticking to these new plans you have help you to live with what you did in a different kind of way?

What way would fit best with you, copping out and just forgetting about these things once you leave here, or turning these things into the journey of a lifetime?

6. **Practice principle six: Acknowledging the gender of the therapist**

The gender of the therapist can be used as a resource in this work. In my case, being a woman therapist, I do this in the following ways:

- By naming any gendered interactions.

- In establishing goals that address the gendered interaction between myself and the client.

- Through celebrating achievements – times of difference in the young man's interaction with me that reflect his commitment to respect and equality.

- By sharing any uncomfortable feelings in a respectful, honest and direct way.

- Through exploring the effects on the young man of having these conversations about masculinity with a woman.

Summary

This paper has endeavoured to explore a relational framework with an associated set of practice principles that guard against the traps and heaviness of totalising ideas and conclusions, particularly in relation to masculinity. This framework assists me to enter into the complexity and diversity of the lived experience of young men. This, in turn, makes it more possible for them to bring forth their genuine struggle as they search for ways to stop abuse and honour their preferred values.

This way of working requires a commitment on my part to listening to young men for evidence of the ways in which the relationships they have with masculinity are informed by multiple competing sets of values, rather than a single set. If young men experience a sense of empowerment to address their struggle between competing masculinities, this opens space for them to achieve their own and the program's objectives of moving towards respectful forms of sexual expression.

I began this paper by describing the heaviness that accompanied my initial engagement with this work. I would like to end it by saying that, as long as I stay on the alert in avoiding totalising ways of thinking about men and masculinity, I now experience this work as very rewarding and energising.

Acknowledgements

I would like to acknowledge the support of my colleagues, close friends and family in the development of my ideas, in particular: Randall Ewens, Geraldine Slattery, Susan Howard, Ian Law, Rob Hall and Alan Jenkins. I would also like to acknowledge the ideas and support of Lesley Porter, who facilitated my workshop at the conference, and the significant editing role that David Denborough played in bringing this paper to its current form.

Notes

This paper was originally published in the *Dulwich Centre Journal*, 2000 Nos.1&2. Republished here with permission. To preserve confidentiality pseudonyms have been used.

1. Ginny Slattery can be contacted c/- Adolescent Sexual Abuse Prevention Program, PO Box 137, Hindmarsh, South Australia 5007, or email: asapp@wch-camhs.sa.gov.au

2. Ryan & Lane (1991) summarise some of these values and attitudes in a helpful way when they discovered similarities between clients attending offending programs. They discovered that young men convicted of sexual offending or sexual harassment often demonstrated:

- Lack of knowledge about positive and consensual sexuality.
- A lack of skills for managing anger, aggression and feelings of powerlessness.
- Acceptance of sex role stereotyping.
- Expression of prevailing, negative social and personal attitudes towards sexuality and power.

References

Bird, J. 1999: 'Just talk.' Two-day workshop, 18th-19th October, BAE Consultants.

Bird, J. 2000: *The Heart's Narrative: Therapy and navigating life's contradictions.* Auckland: Edge Press.

Freedman, J. & Combs, G. 1999: 'Claiming relationships, performing identities' workshop at Dulwich Centre Publications' Narrative Therapy & Community Work Conference, 17th-19th February.

Hall, R. 1996: 'Partnership accountability.' In McLean, C., Carey, M. & White C. (eds): *Men's Ways of Being*, chapter 14. Boulder, Colorado: Westview Press.

Jenkins, A. 1998: 'Invitations to responsibility: Engaging adolescents and young men who have sexually abused.' *Sourcebook of Treatment Programs for Sexual Offenders.* New York: Plenum Press.

Hare-Mustin, R, 1996: 'Foreword.' In McLean, C., Carey, M. & White C. (eds): *Men's Ways of Being.* Boulder, Colorado: Westview Press.

Ryan, G.D. & Lane, S.L. 1991: 'Program development.' In Ryan, G.D. & Lane, S.L. (eds): *Juvenile Sexual Offending: Causes, consequences and correction*, chapter 4. Lexington, MA: Lexington Books.

White, M. 1996: 'Men's culture, the men's movement, and the constitution of men's lives.' In McLean, C., Carey, M. & White C. (eds): *Men's Ways of Being*, chapter 11. Boulder, Colorado: Westview Press.

11.

Groupwork with men who engage in violent and abusive actions

by

Helen Wirtz & Ron Schweitzer[1]

Before we explore in some detail the groups that we facilitate for men who engage in violent and abusive actions, we thought it might be helpful to describe briefly how we have come to be doing this work. In thinking through how to present this work at the conference, we wanted to offer participants a chance to reflect on the diversity of reasons why people choose to work in this area of men's violence. We suspected that many people who would come to listen to our presentation at the conference would have chosen to work in this area for a range of personal and political reasons.

For me (Helen), I developed an interest in working with men around these issues after working with women. So many women with whom I worked had suffered violence and humiliation from their male partners and yet talked of the lovable side of these men, of how they wanted to stay with them, but of how they wanted the violence to stop. The experience of this work made me reflect on issues of gender within the culture and within my own life.

As a young woman I was certainly heavily influenced by the gender specifications of our society. Whilst rebelling against the motto that hung in the assembly hall of the all-female school I attended: 'Be quiet in both speech and movement', I was often troubled by thoughts that maybe my voice was 'too loud' and my demeanour 'too boisterous'. It is for reasons both personal and political that I choose to work with men around issues of violence.

For me (Ron), I can think of two related themes that have led me to be doing this work. The first had to do with coming into contact, during a training course, with ideas about men's violence and abuse, including ideas about patriarchy and men's power. I found the ideas discussed in this training very new and exciting. As a man who considered himself aware of feminist ideas, I rushed home to share the revelations I'd had with Kay (my partner). I thought she would be similarly excited. When I spoke with her, however, her reaction was rather different – she had apparently been trying to talk with me about these issues for the last fifteen years. I had only engaged with them now when they were spoken to me by a man! Despite this shaky start, these ideas have had, and continue to have, a very significant effect on my life in very positive ways. They have in some ways led me to be doing this work with men who are violent. The second theme came from my therapeutic conversations with women, in which time and again I would hear of the violence and abuse that they were being subjected to by their male partners.

Both of us felt a commitment to try to find meaningful ways of addressing the issue of men's violence against their partners. Playing a part in the Men's Responsibility Group has been one of our responses.

The Men's Responsibility Group

The Men's Responsibility Group, which we along with others have been facilitating for the last eleven years, is run for men who engage in violence and abuse at home towards their partner and/or children. The group's primary aim is to maximise the safety of women and children. The men who come to the group are in or have been in heterosexual couple relationships in which the man has been violent and the woman and/or children have been subjected to the man's violence and abuse. This is not to suggest that women are never violent (though in our experience it is the man who is overwhelmingly the perpetrator of violence, and the woman and/or children the recipient of violence). Nor is it to suggest that there is no violence in gay or lesbian relationships. It is just that the Men's Responsibility Group is specifically set up to address violence of men in heterosexual relationships.

There are several components to the Men's Responsibility Group. These include:

1. *A service for men*

   This service involves the groups that are run for men, and may also include individual counselling that is at times offered to the men by one of the facilitators.

2. *A service for women*

   This involves having contact with the women partners of the men before, during and after the men's group. Information groups are also offered to the women on what is happening in the men's program, and any additional contact that the women request is also provided.

3. *A formal reference group*

   We have a formal advisory, managerial and reference group called SCAVA (Southern Collective Against Violence and Abuse) which consists of workers in the field of men's violence and abuse. This includes those who work with women who have been subjected to men's violence and abuse, as well as other interested people.

4. *Teaching/training*

Teaching and training is offered through the opportunity for visitors to sit in and observe the men's groups. The facilitators also offer training sessions and run seminars and workshops.

Here we will describe some of the ideas that inform our work.

Accountability to women and children

As facilitators of The Men's Responsibility Group, we see ourselves as working primarily on behalf of women and children. Our primary aim is to make the lives of women and children safer. These groups are not in any way about the men's 'personal growth', or 'pouring out their hearts', or 'telling their innermost secrets'. Nor is it a 'healing group' for the men. It is a group to address the men's violence and abuse, and to further the safety of women and children. To help ensure that we remain on track in relation to this aim, we have put in place a number of accountability processes.

I. *Partner contact*

In order for a man to join the group it is necessary for him to give us the contact details of his partner/ex-partner. This is because we base any evaluation of the man's progress on the woman's account of how things are going. We always consult with the women on their own. We ring women if the men don't turn up to group meetings, and we invite the women to ring us if they have any concerns or if the men say things about what occurred in the group that they don't believe sound accurate. For example, a member of the group might say to his partner, 'Ron said at the meeting last night that it was okay that I did this or that'. We try to create a context in which the women feel free to contact us and clarify what it is that we have actually said and why.

About every four weeks we invite all the partners along to meet together. In these meetings we go through what we have been talking about in the men's groups. We give the women the handouts we have been using. Some of the men share the handouts with their partners while others keep them very much to themselves. We also show the women the videos that we've been using and catch them up on all that has been happening. Partners are also free to come and sit in on the men's groups if they want to, and a few (not many) choose to do so.[2]

II. *Visitors*

Another accountability practice for the partners and workers is that other workers are invited to sit in on the groups to observe the conversations. We strongly encourage women workers, especially those working with women who have been subjected to violence and abuse, to sit in on the groups so that they can offer us feedback on the ways in which we facilitate the conversations, particularly in relation to our accountability to women. This feedback happens in front of the men in the group. We check with the workers in private if they would be happy to give this feedback, and always state that it is entirely optional and that they shouldn't feel pressured. The workers are also given the opportunity to give feedback after the group has left in case there are things they want to say that they did not feel comfortable to say in the group itself.

III. *Formal reference group*

As mentioned above, we also have a formal reference group (SCAVA) and our consultations with them are a part of our accountability processes.

IV. *Female and male worker*

In working together as a male and female worker, we have our own sense of partnership and accountability. If during a meeting there are differences of opinion as to what area should be explored, there is an upfront acknowledgement that the female worker's opinion will be privileged.

V. *Non-confidentiality*

Although it may seem unusual to some, we facilitate these groups with men with an understanding that what is spoken about is not going to be treated confidentially. This is in line with our position that to take a position against violence at home means taking a position against the silence and secrecy around this sort of violence. We are open with the men from the beginning that what they say in the group may be spoken about in certain situations. We wanted to get away from the idea that what occurred within the men's groups would somehow be 'secret', that there would be things that could be kept from the women partners. As we believe we are running the group on behalf of the partners and children, to keep the conversations secret from them seemed counter-productive.

To our knowledge, most organisations working with men who engage in violent and abusive practices have a protocol in which workers will break confidentiality over issues of safety. We have gone one step further with our non-confidentiality clause. We let the men know that anything they say in the group may be repeated between the facilitators, to the men's partners, and to other relevant workers. We also point out that we can't control what other members of the group will say outside of the groups. We tell the men that if they aren't happy for something to be repeated then they ought not say it in the group. We don't want to have to leave it up to the facilitators' discretion as to what is or what isn't an issue of safety. And we also don't want to say to the men that we will keep things confidential and then not do so.

We are open about the fact that, throughout the duration of the groups, we as facilitators will be having conversations about what is said in the group with the other facilitators (there are five of us involved) and with the partners of the men in the group. Sometimes we also share what has occurred in the group with child protection workers, Office of Corrections people, or other relevant workers. This doesn't happen very often but it can happen and we are open about this. When it does occur that we need to speak to other professionals, we are open with the men in the group about what we have said. Mostly, however, this information-sharing primarily occurs between facilitators and with the partners of the men who are in the group.

We are also transparent about the fact that we have the reverse rule for what the women partners tell us. This remains confidential and will only be shared if these women are happy for us to do so. This is to help ensure the safety of women and children. At times, sharing with the men what their women partners have told us could place these women at risk.

Very occasionally we hear men say that this is not a fair process – that there ought to be the same rule for both the men and their partners. But this is rare. We explain that our thinking behind this policy involves taking a stand against silence and secrecy. We talk about how we believe that, in order to stop violence, we have to stop the silence and secrecy that accompanies it. We are also clear that if any of the men wish to see us individually in therapy, if they wish to speak about experiences that they may have had in childhood for example, then this is a different matter. We make it clear that we are more than happy to see them individually to talk about these issues in a context of confidentiality. But when we are addressing their acts of violence in this group setting, then the structures we have in place are there to prioritise the safety of the women partners. We have undertaken a survey of the men involved in the program to see what they think of this arrangement in regard to confidentiality. From our point of view, as facilitators, it seems to work well. The feedback is that they are accepting of it (with only one or two who say that the non-confidentiality stops them saying some things in the group).

Transparency about where we are coming from – Our golden rules

We are very open about where we are coming from in terms of beliefs about violence and responsibility. We hand out to the group members what we consider to be the 'Golden rules for stopping men's violence and abuse, and being more responsible'.

1. The safety of women and children is always rule number one.

2. No excuses for violence – ever.

3. If you can't challenge the silence and secrecy about violence, you can't stop the violence.

4. Violence is a crime.

5. Violence is a choice.

6. Violence is about using power and control, not about being out of control.

7. If you want to say no to violence, you have to say no to patriarchal thinking.

8. It's the man's responsibility to stop his violence and abuse.

9. Violence and abuse are no laughing matter.

10. If you are responsible, you have the strength to take no for an answer.

11. When you are learning responsibility, the women and children judge your progress.

12. Being responsible means giving up using force and power to get what you want.

Externalising conversations

Within the groups we have many externalising conversations. Sometimes these involve externalising violence directly, other times they involve externalising the 'enemies' and 'friends' of responsibility.

I. *Violence*

We externalise violence by asking men a range of questions about:

- the effects violence is having on their lives, their partners' lives, their children's lives,

- whether violence is taking their life in preferred directions or non-preferred directions,

- what would happen if violence had more of their life,

- what would happen if they got more of their life back from violence.

II. *Enemies of responsibility*

Through externalising conversations, we engage with the men in articulating what they see as the 'enemies of responsibility' – things that get in their way when they are trying to act responsibly. In past groups these have included, but have not been limited to:

- defensiveness

- self-righteousness

- self-centredness

- entitlement notions

- blaming practices

- denial/minimising/trivialising

Once these 'enemies' of responsibility are externalised, they can be referred to throughout the group conversations. For example, if a conversation seems to be getting a bit stuck, we might ask, 'Are any of the enemies of responsibility operating at the moment do people think?'. Different people might then say, 'Oh, it's denial', or it's this and it's that. We are then able to have an externalised conversation about the motives, tactics, and effects of whatever particular enemies of responsibility are present. This enables us, as facilitators, to step outside of policing men's statements. Instead, we can simply ask questions that engage the group in relevant considerations.

We can also set 'homework tasks' in which we invite group members to watch out for any one of the above practices that the group has identified as hindering responsibility and how they can resist them, even if only for short periods of time.

III. *Friends of responsibility*

Friends of responsibility are those practices that the men identify as assisting them to become more responsible and caring. They include, but are not limited to, the following:

- other-centredness
- openness
- caring
- respectfulness
- thoughtfulness
- humility and humbleness

The process of articulating these friends of responsibility can be quite joyful. One group member came up with an entire 'A-Z' list of the friends of responsibility. Once these friends are externalised, we try to explore instances in which the group members have engaged with these friends, what difference it can make to have these friends in their lives and relationships, and ways of inviting these friends more into people's lives.

Documenting unique outcomes

Throughout these discussions, we are interested in articulating and documenting unique outcomes and building alternative stories around the men's preferred ways of being. We create a handout during the sessions that explores the unique outcomes that have been spoken about, the beliefs and values that have informed these unique outcomes and how these may differ from previous ways of being and thinking. This is a little like a group therapeutic document. We also create documents for the individual men that record unique outcomes and their meanings.

Re-membering conversations

As we explore the friends of responsibility, the unique outcomes in men's lives and the alternative stories that may be taking shape, we ask about significant people, men or women in the group members' lives who would be most interested in the journeys they are taking. We ask what these significant people would have said and thought about the changes that these men are trying to make in their lives, and what they would have thought about the steps the group members are taking to engage in more respectful ways of being towards their partners and/or children.

A lot of men in the group have had their own experiences of being subject to violence by their fathers or other men, but there's usually someone whom they know, sometimes even another man, who has been caring and has offered an example of other ways of being. Within the group, we explore these histories in the men's lives and enquire as to what it would be like if the group members could keep more vividly alive the memories of these alternative figures. We ask questions such as: 'If he (the significant person) was talking to you when you were yelling at the kids, what do you think he'd be saying?', or 'If she (significant person) was to know that you were taking these new steps in your life, what would it mean to her?'.

This use of re-membering questions is a relatively new development in our groupwork. We are looking forward to getting more feedback from the men and their partners about its usefulness.

Outsider-witness processes

Within the groups we use outsider-witness processes in a number of ways.

I. *Reflections from other group members*

When a man is telling a different story, a story about an alternative way of being, we often ask other men in the group: 'What is that like for you to hear? What do you think about that?' And the responses that are given are generally very significant to the man doing the telling but also to the group as a whole. We might ask other group members: 'What difference will it make to you this week if you're able to keep what he did or what you've just heard, in your mind? What difference would it make to keep that story alive?' Then we'll return to the man whose story it was and ask: 'What's it like to hear that you might have affected these other men in these ways?'

These reflective processes seem very significant in the group. Again, we are interested in doing some sort of survey to see how the men and their partners have experienced these processes.

II. *Reflections from visitors*

We also involve the visitors in outsider-witness group practices. At the end of each group session, we ask the visitors to share with the group what they will be taking away from the stories they've heard. Sometimes we ask the visitors particular questions, such as: 'Is there anything in particular that you're going to take away from this meeting tonight? Were there any aspects of the discussion tonight that will influence the work you do, or the conversations you share with others?'

We have to take care with this process because sometimes the visitors who are sitting in on the groups are nervous about attending. This is particularly true for some women who work with women who have been abused. We try to take care when inviting the visitors to speak by ensuring they are not put on the spot. We might say something like: 'If you don't want to say anything that's fine, we don't want to put pressure on you, but we were just wondering if you'd like to offer some reflections on what you have heard today.'

III.*Reflections from facilitators*

Sometimes one of the facilitators will share the effects on them of hearing the stories that have been told within the group, and what these stories have evoked in terms of thoughts about their own life and work.

Internalised other questioning

One of the aspects of the group that the visitors often comment upon is when we use 'internalised-other interviewing'. We interview the men as if they were their partners. We ask them questions and they answer as if they were speaking in their partner's voice, from their perspective. We do this specifically when we're having a session on the effects of the abuse on their partners. We ask questions such as:

Addressing Jack (whose partner is Jill):

Jill, can you tell us a bit about what it was like when Jack ... What were you thinking? What were you hoping? What effect did it have on you? What effect did it have on the relationship?

We have found this process helpful in inviting men to step into the shoes of their partners. It is often an intensely emotional experience. Many of the men are tearful in this part of the group, particularly when they endeavour to represent their partner's experience of fear and sadness. We've had feedback from the women partners that this has had a powerful effect on the men. Often it has been after this session that the men have come home and apologised. It can be a starting point for these men in opening themselves to their partner's experience of them.

Recent changes and surveys

To end this paper, we want to describe some of the recent changes we have made to the ways in which the groups are run, and the results of surveys that were undertaken during 1999 about these changes.

I. *Visitors and their contribution*

We have always had visitors sit in on our groups as part of our practices of accountability. And yet, we have always wondered what impact these visitors have on the men's experience of the group. Other workers had told us that having visitors sit in on the groups would have terrible effects, particularly for the group members. Although from our observation this didn't seem to be the case, we began to feel concerned about the presence of visitors and so we conducted a survey in which we asked the group members about this.

In our first survey, all the men answered 'yes' to the statement: 'Having the visitors is a good thing', and 'no' to the statement: 'I don't say what I want to say because of the visitors'. We were pleasantly surprised by this result. The only negative comment we received about the visitors was: 'We don't like it if they don't say anything'. The significance of this comment was reinforced to me (Ron) a few months ago when I was running a group and a new member didn't say anything for the entire duration of the group – even when he was asked a question. This silence was scary for me because I didn't know what he was thinking. This really brought home to me the importance of the visitors contributing during the session, so that the men can have an idea of what the visitors are thinking. The visitors are now invited to contribute during the session, and we provide some time at the completion of the evening for them to offer their reflections.

II. *Moving towards an open group with rotating facilitators*

Since 1992 we had run two distinct groups each year. The groups were run weekly for 12 to 15 weeks, with monthly follow-up for the next 3 to 6 months. Each group was run by the same two facilitators (a male and a female).

Recently though we became increasingly aware of the limitations of this model:

1. If a man missed the beginning of a group, there was a long wait before they could commence another. Many men who had to wait so long would lose interest before the next group began.
2. Often group members moved during the course of the group or the follow-up and so we could no longer contact them.

3. Pressure would be placed on the facilitators to have to commit to weekly meetings for 12 to 15 weeks plus ongoing commitment for the follow-up groups.

4. The groups generally had a drop-out rate of approximately a third by the fourth week. This can result in a loss of morale, energy and motivation to change for the men remaining in the group. It also means that the resources being put into the groups only reach a small number of men. If the groups start with 12 (and this is a good number for the groups), there may only be 6-8 members in the last few weeks.

In response to these limitations, we made two significant changes. Firstly, we moved from having a closed group structure to an open ongoing group that men can join at any point (after having had an initial interview and having signed an agreement). Secondly, we decided that, rather than having the same two facilitators each week, we would rotate facilitators each 6 or 8 weeks (always one man, one woman).

Moving to an open group structure has meant that a man can ring up, receive an appointment with one of the facilitators, and attend his first group meeting within one to two weeks which was previously not possible. This has been a significant improvement but we did have concerns about how an open group membership would affect group cohesion. How would it work if men were at different stages in thinking about the issues? Would it matter that men did not start at the 'beginning' and proceed through to the 'end' of the program?

We also had some initial concerns about rotating facilitators. We worried that this too might have a negative effect on group cohesion, especially as the facilitators wouldn't know the men so well.

In order to see if our concerns were justified, last year we carried out surveys with the men about these changes. We were very surprised and pleased with the results. The men, almost universally, endorsed the changes and commented on the positive effect some of these changes have had – some of which we would never have been able to predict.

No-one had any negative comments of the visitors being in the group, in fact, group members found their presence to be 'good' and 'helpful'. Having different facilitators was also seen in a positive light as it offered different ideas, thoughts and perspectives. Having new men continually joining the groups was also experienced positively as they also brought 'new ideas'.[2]

We would be very interested in hearing from other practitioners who are working with therapeutic groups that involve visitors, open group membership, and rotating facilitators. We will continue to conduct surveys to look at the impact, positive or negative, that these changes are having on the group processes. We see our work with the Men's Responsibility Group as a continually evolving practice and we would welcome feedback, suggestions and ideas.

Acknowledgements

The Men's Responsibility Group described in this article is proudly sponsored by Tattersalls. We wish to acknowledge and thank all those women who gave us their trust and shared their experiences with us. They encouraged us to embark on this program and to continue. We acknowledge also the thoughts and comments from those men in our groups who have contributed to the development of our ideas and of the program. We wish to acknowledge the enormous contribution to our work made by Ron Findlay. Ron has been a constant source of ideas, knowledges and inspiration in our work. We would also like to acknowledge the contribution of the following people to the ideas in this article: Michael White, David Epston, Alan Jenkins, Kay Schweitzer, Gael Wallace, Jo Howard, Andrea Rhodes-Little, Shane Weir, Eddie Gallagher, John Ward, and David Denborough.

Notes

This paper was originally published in the *Dulwich Centre Journal*, 2000 Nos.1&2. Republished here with permission.

1. Helen Wirtz is a social worker and family therapist working at MonashLink Community Health Service. Ron Schweitzer is a doctor and family therapist in private practice. Both live and work in a suburb of Melbourne, Victoria, Australia. Helen can be contacted at MonashLink Community Health Service, PO Box 74, Chadstone, Victoria 3748, Australia, email: wirtz@optusnet.com.au Ron Schweitzer can be contacted at 1123 North Road, Oakleigh, Victoria 3166, Australia, email: schweitzer@blaze.net.au

2. Providing the opportunity for women to sit in on the men's group as witnesses to the conversation has occasionally created a bit of a dilemma as it is important that women partners are not pressured into doing so. Sometimes a woman might say, 'Well, the only way he'll come is if I sit in, so I want to come'! We might reply, 'But we don't want you to be forced'. When they say they are not being forced it can be a bit tricky to know what to do, but this situation does not happen often.

12.

Dichotomies in the Power and Control Story:

Exploring multiple stories about men who choose abuse in intimate relationships

by
Tod Augusta-Scott[1]

Introduction

For a number of years I have worked with men who have used violence against their female partners, and during this time I have utilised the power and control story as a grand narrative to explain the entirety of battering. The power and control story states that men *want* power and control, *use* power and control ('tactics'), and *get* power and control by abusing their female partners (Pence & Paymar 1993; Paymar 2000; Emerge 2000). The power and control story is told through the Power and Control Wheel (Pence & Paymar 1993). Gradually, however, I have recognised how the power and control story as a grand narrative is often unable to account for the multiple, complex, and often contradictory stories men tell me about their abusive behaviour.[2] Many of these stories (along with the power and control story) seem important to address in ending battering. Some of these other stories involve men's desires for loving and respectful relationships, men's experiences of injustice and powerlessness, men's shame, and men's fears. Believing in the significance of the power and control story, I did not acknowledge the importance of any other stories. In hindsight, I believe this was in part due to the influence of dichotomous thinking. Dichotomous thinking restrained me from accepting stories that contradict the power and control story. As well, I did not notice how both my practice and how I defined the men within the power and control grand narrative were being influenced by dominant masculinity.

More recently, I have begun to use the therapeutic approach developed by Alan Jenkins (1990, 1991, 1994, 1996, 1997, 1998). Through using this therapeutic approach, I have moved away from dichotomous thinking and toward identifying in my work the importance of the multiple, complex, and contradictory stories about battering.[3] As well, I have been able to weaken the influence of dominant masculinity on both my intervention practice and how I define those with whom I work. This article draws on my own experiences as well as qualitative research I have conducted with other counsellors who use the power and control story in their work with men who batter (Augusta-Scott 1999).[4]

Historical context

The power and control story developed from the efforts of the battered women's movement to challenge the prevailing mental health and legal responses to battering. Often therapeutic interventions with battering were perceived as colluding with the men not taking responsibility for their abusive behaviour. Rather than focusing men on taking responsibility to stop their abuse, therapeutic interventions were seen as exacerbating a man's irresponsible stories by suggesting that his abuse is *caused* by his female partner, abuse in his childhood, 'impulse control disorder', low self-esteem, alcohol, and so forth. In contrast, the power and control story focused on both the intentionality of the men's abusive behaviour and the men's responsibility to stop it. The power and control story informed the development of education groups (as opposed to therapy groups) which were designed to hold men accountable and responsible for their abusive behaviour. Therapy was said to ignore the significance of the gender stories as well as individualise, pathologise, and de-politicise the issue of men's violence against women. In contrast, the power and control grand narrative was meant to politicise the issue and highlight the significant influence of the traditional gender stories on battering (Pence & Shepard 1999).

The battered women's movement also saw the legal system as unresponsive to women who were abused by their partners. This unresponsiveness was interpreted as an indication of how communities collude with men who batter. By emphasising the intentionality of the abuse and the men's responsibility for it, the battered women's movement used the power and control story to mobilise communities to hold the men accountable and responsible for their actions through the legal system (Pence & Shepard 1999).

The power and control story was developed from the experiences of women who have been abused by their male partners. The battered women's movement identified the importance of including the stories of these women in defining the problem of battering. In particular the movement identified the importance of intervention work with men needing to be accountable to female partners and their stories of the abuse. As a result, many of the intervention programs hold themselves accountable to the female partners by contacting them directly to hear about their experiences of the abuse and any changes that may be happening while the man is in the program (Pence & Shepard 1999).

The work of the battered women's movement, and its attention to relations of power and issues of accountability have changed the shape of responses to men's violence in many positive ways. Our understanding of these issues has been changed dramatically. Workers and communities are now engaged in thinking through how to avoid colluding in men's violence because of the work of the battered women's movement.

I engaged with the power and control story because of commitments that I share in common with the battered women's movement. I maintain these commitments. In this paper I wish to explore some of the unintended consequences of understanding men's violence solely through the power and control story, and some alternatives which I am currently exploring. One of the unintended consequences of the power and control story is that it can obscure the multiple desires that men who batter have for their lives and relationships.

Stories of men's desires

The power and control grand narrative states that men batter because they *want* power and control. Along with many of the counsellors I interviewed, I have used the power and control story to explain battering. In so doing, workers define the men in terms of wanting power and control over their partners. When asked what men are wanting to achieve through battering, one of the workers, Dorothy, responded:

Maintaining power and control, that's why they batter and that's how they maintain it, to keep it. They don't want to let it go, they want to be in charge, they want to be the boss and they want to have power over somebody at all cost to themselves, to their partner, to their children. And sometimes it sounds that easy and if we could spell it out that easy but it's really hard for them to get that and understand that.

While Alan Jenkins (1990) notices men's desires for power and control, he also identifies men's desires for relationships based on love, respect, and closeness. Jenkins (1996) states, 'Most of the men I see are not wanting relationships in which they abuse those whom they love. I believe that their preferred ways of being and relating are respectful and equitable, despite their disrespectful practices' (p.120).

Following this, I have begun to explore the multiple stories of men's desires. Of course, just because a man *says* he wants love, respect, and equality in a relationship, I do not assume that he has an immediate and profound understanding of these ideas and practices. Naming these values is a starting point. The men will spend the rest of their time in the program exploring the complexity and importance of these ideas to developing intimate relationships. Jenkins (1990) writes:

> *Whilst I respect the man's argument for non-violence and mutuality, I do not regard them as evidence of his readiness to cease violence or engage new behaviour. They are regarded as a point of reference which he has provided and to which the therapist can return throughout therapy and compare and contrast the man's actions. I am not concerned about the 'truth' of the arguments – whether they are true representations of his feelings, socially desirable responses or attempts to deceive the therapist. I regard them as beginning steps towards responsibility and integrity and invite the man to entertain these ideas in a variety of ways.* (p.72)

I have come to believe that in the process of challenging men's violence, noticing men's desires for relationships based on love, respect, and caring is important. Often by naming these desires the men experience themselves as resisting traditional masculine ideas about men only wanting power and control and not caring about love and respect. For example, in an early group session I invite the men to identify their relationship desires and I put them on a flip chart. In one particular group, after the flip chart paper was almost filled with many of the men's desires such as trust, respect and so forth, a large man cautiously said, 'I want ... *love* in my relationship'. The man was cautious because he thought the other men in the group might shame him for wanting 'love' in his relationship. Instead, the group recognised his courage in standing up to the traditional masculine script.

In noticing men's multiple desires, it is then possible to invite the men to notice how their desires for love, respect, and intimacy are thwarted by abusive practices and sexist beliefs about relationships. The men can then evaluate for themselves if abusive behaviour is achieving the loving and close relationship they want. Through the process of noticing these other stories about men's desires and evaluating their practices, men can become self-motivated to change.

Dichotomous thinking led me and my co-workers to believe that men want either power and control *or* love and equality. In contrast, Jenkins notices that often the men's desires are contradictory. Men often want *both* power over their partners *and* equal, respectful relationships at the same time. Focusing on men's desire for love and respect does not mean that men do not also want power and control in their relationships. Dichotomous thinking prevented me from noticing the complexity and contradictions in the men's desires. To maintain the power and control story, dichotomous thinking led me to dismiss men's desires for respect and love which contradict this story. When men would say they loved their partners or children, we believed they were insincere and simply trying to avoid responsibility for their 'real' intentions of wanting power and control.

By negating men's desires for loving and close relationships, the grand narrative of power and control may inadvertently replicate dominant masculinity by insisting these men only care about power and control and do not care about respectful, caring relationships. As well, in retrospect, I never realised how my implicit (and often explicit) assumptions about the men's desires (i.e., that they wanted power and control and were not concerned about the well being of their children or partner) often fuelled the men's anger toward myself. This anger was defined as the men's 'denial' and 'control tactics' in their efforts to mask their desires for power and control. Avoiding dichotomous thinking, and being open to the multiplicity of men's desires, is creating new options for collaborating with men in addressing their abusive actions.

The abuse 'working' and 'not working'

The power and control story states that men not only *want* power and control but they also *use* power and control ('tactics') and *get* the effects (i.e., power and control) they want through battering. Early in the intervention process, men often avoid taking responsibility for their calculating, intentional, and deliberate *use* of abusive behaviour (e.g., many men say, 'I just lost it' or 'I was out of control'). To hold the men responsible for their intentional *use* of abuse, we used the power and control story to emphasise that the abuse is calculated, they 'didn't just loose it', and were not 'out of control'. Toward this end, the men's abuse was defined as 'control tactics' (Pence & Paymar 1993). As well, early in the intervention process, men often avoid taking responsibility for the effects of the abuse (e.g., many men say, 'I didn't mean it'). To hold the men responsible for the intended effects they *get* from the abuse (i.e., power and control), we used the power and control story to insist that the men 'did mean it', that they did get what they wanted from the abuse. We emphasised the intended effects of the abuse and de-emphasised the unintended effects. To emphasis the intended effects of the abuse, we described what the men *get* from the abuse in terms of 'payoffs', 'benefits', and 'privileges' (Pence & Paymar 1993; Paymar 2000). Further to this, to emphasise both the calculated *use* of abuse and the intended effects the men *get* from it, we defined the abuse as 'working'. One of the workers I interviewed, Kirk, reported:

> *Men batter because it works. It works. It works to get them what they want. I*
> *believe abuse can be reduced down to two reasons: one reason is you want to*
> *make your partner do something, the other reason is you want to stop her*
> *from doing something. The bottom line is it works.*

Dichotomous thinking led me and my co-workers to believe that the violence must be considered as either calculated or not calculated; either the effects are intentional or unintentional; the men either 'mean it' or 'do not mean it'; the abuse was either 'working' or 'not working'. While Jenkins (1990) also only emphasises the calculated and intentional *use* of abuse,[5] in terms of the effects the men *get* from the abuse, he finds it helpful to emphasise how the abuse might *both* 'work' *and* 'not work' at the same time. Jenkins invites the men to notice the ways in which they are *not* achieving what they want through using violence in their intimate relationships. The men are encouraged to notice how the abuse is taking them away from the loving and respectful relationships they want. Through inviting the man to notice how the abuse is *not* working, the counselors can create a context in which the man is more likely to develop self-motivation to end the abuse.

Jenkins (1990) identifies how men's 'power and control tactics' often reflect a man's misguided attempts to build a relationship that is respectful and loving. To get their relationships to 'work', these men often follow the traditional gender stories they have had told to them (i.e., men are to work outside the home, be rational, make decisions while women are to make the relationships in the family 'work' by being the emotional care takers, peace keepers, and nurture relationships). These traditional gender stories often act as a recipe that men and women are influenced by to achieve caring and respectful relationships. This recipe is often misguided and does not lead people to the relationships they want. As a result of this misguided recipe, when the relationship is *not* working and he is abusive, he *blames* her for not being nurturing enough or for not being the peace keeper. If the woman is influenced by these traditional gender stories, she will also blame herself for his abuse and the relationship failing. When the relationship is not working, the man's misguided attempts to fix it often involve trying to control her, to get her to live up to her responsibilities. Jenkins (1990) invites the men to notice how this 'misguided recipe' does not actually lead to the respectful, caring relationships they want.

The result of primarily emphasising the idea that men are *getting* what they want by beating their female partners (i.e., men are achieving the power and control they desire) led myself and my coworkers to be pessimistic about the men ever changing. We inadvertently smothered the men's motivation to change by insisting that their violence was 'working' to get them what they 'want'. Believing the men had little motivation to change, we believed we had to be in opposition to the men, challenging and confronting them to change. This dynamic was often fuelled further by implicit dichotomies in our intervention that suggested the workers were good, the men were bad; that workers were right, the men were wrong, and so forth.

Dichotomous thinking led us to negate any possible contradictions between the men's desires and the *effects* of their violence. Rather than accepting that there may be a contradiction between men's desires for respectful relationships and the effects of their violence, we inferred the men were being dishonest about their respectful intentions. To maintain the idea that the violence was calculated and 'working' to get them what they want, we implicitly suggested that the men knew 'exactly what they are doing'. We implied that there were no unintended or unwanted effects of the abuse. (While implying the men knew 'exactly what they are doing', at the same time, we invited the men to study the effects of their violence. In retrospect, I recognise that, presumably, if the men knew 'exactly what they were doing', they would not have to study the effects of their violence – they would already know them. This contradiction in the approach may have created confusion for the men.) While the men's behavior is often calculated, in terms of the effects of the abuse, they often *both* 'know what they are doing' (e.g., winning an 'argument') *and* 'do not know what they are doing' (e.g., destroying their relationships) at the same time. Often they both 'mean it' (i.e., intend the effects) and 'do not mean it' (i.e., do not intend the effects of their violence). After being asked what difference it made to study the effects of the abuse on his partner and children, one of the men in my group, Daniel, explained:

> *I don't think I ever accidentally said anything in my life to hurt somebody. If I said something to hurt somebody, I said it because I wanted to hurt them. However, to be able to feel how bad they felt and how bad I hurt them gives me a real perspective on what I've done, the pain I've caused, and the damage I've done ... I didn't realise how bad it was. I was doing it to win, I was going to win ... All I was winning was driving people away from me.*

Daniel describes both knowing and not knowing the effects of his abuse. He describes 'meaning it' and 'not meaning it'. He illustrates the calculated nature of the abuse, while at the same time illustrating the un-calculated effects. Acknowledging these complexities allows workers to join with a man's respectful intentions, to emphasis how the abuse is 'not working' as a means of developing a man's self-motivation to stop it, and to invite him to take responsibility for the effects of his abuse whether he intended them or not.

Stories of power and powerlessness

Consistent with the story of abuse 'working', the power and control grand narrative defines the men as having power and control. Dichotomous thinking leads counsellors to believe that a person is either powerful or powerless and prevents workers from considering that the men are often *both* powerful *and* powerless at the same time. Often men do have power and control in these relationships. At the same time, the power and control story prevented us from noticing men's experiences of powerlessness both inside and outside of their intimate relationships.

Inside their intimate relationship, many men only achieve a momentary feeling of power and control through beating their female partners. Often the feeling of power and control is fleeting, and is quickly followed by feelings of shame, self-disgust, and powerlessness to change their relationships or themselves. As well, many of the men I work with experience an extreme emotional and social dependency on their female partners. Many men in desperation will say, 'she's all I've got'. Men's emotional and social dependency on their female partners often leads to feelings of powerlessness over their own emotional life and their relationships with others (Jenkins 1990). The power and control story helps counsellors notice how intimate relationships are sites of power for men, but the same story prevented us from noticing how intimate relationships are also sites of powerlessness. By defining men primarily as powerful and in control, the power and control story seems to risk replicating dominant masculinity by ignoring men's experiences of powerlessness.

Often women experience their partners as both powerful and powerless. However, for women who may only experience him as powerful (as the power and control grand narrative suggests), he may still experience himself as powerless at the same time. There may be a contradiction between how she is experiencing him and how he is experiencing himself. Talking about his feelings of powerlessness, does not dismiss or negate that she may experience him as very powerful. Both experiences may happen at the same time. Often the men and women have very different experiences of their relationship. Dichotomous thinking leads counselors to believe they must validate as 'true' either the men's story or the women's story. That there are different experiences of the relationship does not mean counselors have to choose to validate one over the other. Both experiences can be acknowledged. As we confront the complexity of ending abuse, often it is important to notice many of these seemingly conflicting stories. I have found that noticing the men's experiences of reliance, dependency and powerlessness in their intimate relationships is important in having men end their abuse (Jenkins 1990; Kane, Staiger & Ricciardelli 2000). Having the men move away from the social expectations of relying on their female partners to meet the men's own social-emotional responsibilities can be important in ending abuse. Having the men take responsibility for their own emotional and social independence within an intimate relationship gives them a sense of power and control over their own feelings and relationships. This experience of power and control seems to decrease the abuse. By ignoring men's dependency on women, the power and control story seems to risk replicating dominant masculinity in masking men's dependency on women and 'women's work' in the lives of men.

By defining the men as powerful and not powerless, the dichotomous thinking informing the power and control story also prevented us from accounting for the men's experiences of powerlessness and injustice outside of their intimate relationships.[6] Many of the men I work with are marginalised by poverty, racism, and lack of access to education. Many of these men do not experience beating their female partners as resulting in any type of sustainable 'power' and 'privilege'. The power and control story may create dissonance and alienation for many of these men. The power and control story informed by dichotomous thinking kept me from noticing that battering often leads these men to feel even further marginalised (McKendy 1997, p.168).

One of the workers I interviewed, Kirk, noticed the dissonance between the power and control story and the lived experiences of many of the men with whom he works. Kirk states:

> *In group I talk about differences in power and racial differences and I lay that out on the line. Not as much as I think would be good most of the time, but as much as I can do comfortably. I'm white, I'm approaching middle age, and I'm usually working with younger black men. Often it doesn't feel appropriate or comfortable as I'm talking to them about power because they are the ones who experience blatant disempowerment by society, they aren't hired for jobs, they are targeted for violence by groups of white men or non-black men, the legal system enforces the law to the max on these guys, the stereotypes abound, and expectations of illegal or illicit behavior follow them everywhere they go. All this stuff is racism, the subtle expectations, the comments, the subtle put downs, always pointing out the difference between them and us.*

Kirk illuminates the tension of simply describing the outcome of battering as 'power and control', especially for men who are oppressed by racism and poverty. He notices the complexity of battering when the power and control story is accompanied by stories of racism and poverty.

Responding to the men's experiences of injustice and powerlessness

Early in the intervention process, men often avoid responsibility for their abuse by blaming it on their experiences of powerlessness and injustice (i.e., poverty, racism, childhood violence, and so forth). When men blame external factors for their abuse, rather than taking responsibility themselves, it seems important to interrupt these irresponsible stories from being told. If programs allow these stories to be told in ways that lessen a man's sense of responsibility for his violence, then this may run the risk of colluding with the man's violence. When I was using the power and control story informed by dichotomous thinking, however, I did not identify any value in the stories men might share of their own experiences of injustice and powerlessness. I saw no way in which these could be relevant in ending the men's violence. These stories contradicted the power and control story. As a result, I often excluded these stories from the change process. Men's experiences of childhood violence, poverty, and racism were all excluded from the change process. Focussing on men's pain, powerlessness, and experiences of injustice was seen as risking excusing the men's behaviour.

In contrast, while Jenkins similarly interrupts stories of injustice and powerlessness if they are being told in an irresponsible manner to excuse the abuse, he also identifies that stories of injustice and stories of powerlessness can be told in a manner that avoids excusing irresponsible behaviour. In fact, Jenkins identifies how such stories can be told in a responsible manner which can be very helpful to end abuse. For example, often within men's stories of their past exist many examples of the men standing up against injustice. Many of the men with whom I work have tried to stop their fathers from beating their mothers. Noticing these experiences where the men have demonstrated their preference for justice helps to 're-story' the men facing their own abuse and taking responsibility for it as consistent with their own preferences. Studying past abuse they have experienced, can also help men understand the current impact of their own abusive behavior. As well, one of the effects of creating a context for men to be able to speak of their own experiences of injustice is that it enables the counselor to model for the man ways of listening and acknowledging the effects of abuse. This is significant because it may enable the man to realise the significance of being open to listening to his partner's experiences of his abuse.

In the past I excluded men's stories of injustice and powerlessness from my conversations with men because dichotomous thinking led me and my co-workers to define the men as either perpetrators or victims. As a result, we did not know how to think about and respond to the men as *both perpetrators* of violence against their partners *and*, at the same time, as people who have been *victims* of violence, poverty, racism, and so forth. I think we were also reluctant to notice how the men were victimised because a 'victim' is defined as someone who is not responsible and who is without agency (Mahoney 1994).[7] Within this framework, we thought to hold the men responsible, we could not talk about them as victims in any way.[8] Moving away from dichotomous thinking is allowing me to notice how men are often both perpetrators and victims, powerful and powerless, and *responsible* for their abuse all at the same time. I also neglected men's experiences of powerlessness and injustices because I did not realise how these stories can be helpful in ending the men's own violence (Jenkins, 1998). I thought the only way the men would or could tell these stories was in an irresponsible manner to excuse their abusive behaviour. We did not know how to invite men to tell these stories responsibly in a way which would lead to them taking more responsibility for their own violence. One of the workers I interviewed, Derrick, reported struggling with the victim/perpetrator dichotomy and his desire to move beyond it:

I think we really need to integrate working with men as victim and perpetrator. I would hope we would be able to find healthier ways of being able to integrate both of them. Drawing on men's experience of victimisation and using that to be empathetic and to understand the impact of their behavior on their victims. I haven't done it, but I think that would be more holistic. Otherwise we are separating his experiences as victim and perpetrator and there needs to be some integration ... I'm not sure how to do that.

By only focusing on men as perpetrators, the dichotomous thinking in the power and control story may replicate dominant masculinity by insisting men are not victims, not powerless, and do not feel pain.

Stories of men's shame

By suggesting that men get what they want through battering, the power and control story led us to believe that men do not feel shame over their violence. There is no reason to believe the men would feel shame over battering since, so the story goes, the men only get what they want, they 'like it' (Jones 1994), and they believe battering is 'their right' (Pence & Paymar 1993; Paymar 2000; Emerge 2000). When men 'minimise' the serious of the abuse and 'deny' it, these actions are defined solely as 'control tactics' that the men use to maintain power over their partners. As a result, I and my co-workers often adopted an oppositional relationship with the men by confronting and challenging their 'minimising and denial' (Pence & Paymar 1993; Paymar 2000; Emerge 2000). As well, the men's explicit displays of remorse, shame, and pain over their violence were seen as insincere or simply reflecting the man's self-pity. They were seen as attempts to get sympathy but not engage in change.

In the past, I did not attend to men's shame in relation to their violence in part because I had adopted an anti-therapeutic position (Mederos 1999). Approaches which focused on the men's shame were constructed as therapeutic, and in my mind this represented colluding with the violence. The power and control story defines the men's displays of shame as 'control tactics' that the men use to manipulate not only their partners but also the counselors. Focusing on the men's shame in a therapeutic manner was understood as colluding with the men · in defining themselves as victims (i.e., not responsible). I did not know how to respond to the men's shame and hold them responsible at the same time. In contrast, Jenkins (1990) notices that many men who batter often feel both entitled to have power (i.e., no shame) and, at the same time, feel shame over their violence. Jenkins suggests that when men 'minimise and deny' their violence this can have the effect of creating irresponsible stories and yet, at the same time, the 'minimising and denying' can also be evidence of the men feeling shame and remorse over their violence. Many of the men have learned that it is not acceptable to 'hit a woman'. Jenkins (1994) states:

> *When men who have abused begin to accept responsibility for their actions, they face powerful feelings of shame, sadness, and fear, as they begin to think and feel about the harm they have caused and the damage they have done to the ones they love.* (p.15)

Jenkins (1998) also writes:

> *They demonstrate considerable minimization of the abuse and accept little responsibility for their actions. These men are often frightened of the likely consequences of their actions, and their avoidant and minimizing*

behaviour masks a profound and pervasive sense of shame. They expect deprecation from others and feel little respect for themselves. Their assaults and subsequent apprehension confirm to themselves that they are 'losers' whose only option is to run and hide from what they have done and what they think it says about them. (p.165)

In contrast to the counsellor being oppositional and confrontational toward the men's 'minimisation and denial', Jenkins respectfully interrupts the irresponsible stories and at other times 'normalises' the men's minimising and denial as evidence of their shame (Jenkins 1998). He invites the men to consider their shame as evidence that the men do not like their violence, that they are not relating in a manner that fits with what they want for their families.

Stories of men's fears

Questioning dichotomous thinking has also led us to consider men's experiences of 'fear' in this work. In these considerations, it requires care not to conflate the fear and safety issues of women who are subject to men's physical violence on a regular basis, with the fear and safety issues of men who abuse. I do believe, however, that it is relevant for us as workers who are engaging with men who use violence, to consider these men's experiences of 'fear' and 'safety'.[9] To do so is to challenge the dominant gender stories that suggests that men have 'no fear'. It also has practical implications as to how we conduct our work with men.

The power and control story also suggests that the men are not afraid and, in fact, due to their power and control, they feel safe in the world. Only the female partner feels afraid and unsafe. As a result of believing the men felt safe and were not afraid, in the past we did not see a problem with holding groups with large numbers of men that were open to new members every week. In contrast, Jenkins (1998) suggests that often, men who are violent to their partners are afraid. The men are not only afraid of losing their partners, they are afraid of what the abuse might say about them, how they will be treated, and what others will think of them. As well, many of these men have experienced violence and are fearful of other men, especially other men who have been identified as violent. As a result, to address the men's fears, we now have small groups that are not open to new members every week. One of the counsellors I interviewed, Derrick, reflects on not noticing men's fear:

> *I think men's fear of other men is something we don't talk about or look at. We kind of plop these men together and we never stop and ask 'what was it like for you in the beginning to be with a group of men?'... I think there is lots going on the first night when they are with twenty men. I think it must blow their minds ... we never try to engage them to look at that whole thing.*

Another worker who was interviewed, Sarah, who uses the power and control story, also reports not noticing the men's fears. She reports:

> *I never thought about men fearing men. That may very well be. Sometimes we have men in group who do not speak for the first three or four group sessions and we have to draw every word out of them. Maybe that is because they are afraid of who is in the group. Some men name they are shy. That's how they define it. Whether that is out of fear or not I don't know. It will be interesting to explore that. And I think that the men who are really talkative may be talkative as a way of dealing with the fear. Fear of someone having more power than them ... The men want to make known who they are and what their presence is. Their territory is marked ... 'I'm the big guy and you're going to listen to me'.*

By ignoring men's fear and shame, the power and control story may risk replicating dominant masculinity in suggesting that men have 'no fear' or pain.

Responding to men's fears

Dichotomous thinking also led me and my co-workers to believe that we must create an intervention which is either respectful of the women *or* respectful of the men; that would be sensitive to women's experiences *or* men's experiences; that will meet either women's interests or men's interests. As a result, we believed that providing emotional safety for men would mean putting women in danger. For example, a counsellor of the intervention program

'Emerge', David Adams (1988) criticises using a non-threatening therapeutic approach (rather than a confrontational approach) because 'taking the time to create a safe environment for the batterer can sometimes mean perpetuating an unsafe environment for his partner' (p.181).

In contrast, Jenkins (1998) suggests that intervention can be and needs to be respectful and safe for both women and men. We do not have to choose between men's interests and women's interests: putting the 'victim's safety first' by stopping a man from beating his female partner is in *both* their interests. My co-workers and I also ignored men's fear of other men because we were focused solely on men's violence *against women* and thought that men's violence against men was unrelated (Schecter 1982, p.210). In contrast, a range of writers (Kaufman 1987; Goldner et al. 1990) have articulated the ways in which men's violence against other men plays a significant part in constructing dominant forms of masculinity and as such is directly linked to men's violence against women.

Dominant constructions of masculinity support and enable a variety of practices of domination including men's violence against women, men's violence against other men, homophobia, and practices of competition. It is my belief, that in order to stop battering, we need to find ways of challenging all these practices of domination. Within the groups we run for men who have been violent to their female partners, alongside our conversations about taking responsibility for this violence, we have also begun to talk about the effects of men's violence against men, competition, and homophobia. One of the ways in which we do this is by inviting the men in the group to talk about their fears of other men in group. By naming their fears and creating safety guidelines to assist in this process, men experience a context in which they can risk exploring new ways of being. I believe this is assisting participants in the group to step into new ways of being men.[10] The process of inviting the men to consider what safety means for themselves can begin a process of the men considering what safety might mean for their female partners. Again, I am careful not to equate the idea of safety for the men with safety for the women.

In retrospect, by trivialising and ignoring men's fear and the effects of men's violence against men, our intervention in the past may have often replicated dominant masculinity. One of the effects of not noticing men's fear of other men and running large, open groups was that a threatening environment was created. This context stimulated the 'minimising, denying, and blaming' the men sometimes use in relation to their violence, both to abdicate responsibility and also to cover their fear and shame. Unfortunately, we would then respond to the men's minimising and denial by confronting and challenging them. We defined the men's minimising and denial solely in terms of 'control tactics' that they could simply 'drop' whenever they were willing to give up their power and control, and ignored how their expressions of minimising could be related to shame or regret. While we believed that confronting the men's minimising and denial would lessen it, often our confrontation would lead to an increase in minimising and denial because inadvertently we were adding to the shame and fear it was masking. We did not notice how the very group process we put the men in (i.e., large, open groups which involved oppositional confrontation) was stimulating the very behaviour and dangerous, irresponsible stories we were trying to stop. By not noticing men's fear and engaging the men with oppositional, confrontational and competitive practices, we may replicate the very masculine practices we are trying to change in the men with whom we work (Jenkins 1993).

Conclusion

Using research interviews with those who work with men who batter and my experiences in the field, this article has sought to identify how dichotomous thinking informs the power and control grand narrative and precludes other stories which are important to notice in stopping battering. These other stories include the men's desires for power and control as well as respectful and loving relationships, the violence 'working' and 'not working', the men's experiences of power as well as powerlessness and injustice, the men's entitlement and shame over their violence, and the men's fears. Finally, this article reflects a painful process of noticing how I have often replicated in my work with men who batter the same masculine practices and assumptions which I am trying to change. My intention is to reflexively question my practices and assumptions in the same way I am inviting the men I work with to question theirs.

Notes

This paper was originally published in *Gecko: a journal of deconstruction and narrative ideas in therapeutic practice,* 2001 No.2. Republished here with permission.

1. Tod Augusta-Scott, MSW is the program coordinator of Bridges – A Domestic Abuse Intervention Program, Truro, Nova Scotia, Canada. He is a counsellor for men who choose abuse in intimate relationships and is a sessional instructor at the Social Work Department, Dalhousie University. He also works as a consultant and trainer on the issue of battering for both government and non-government agencies. Mr. Augusta-Scott has conducted research on domestic violence and made presentations to international audiences. He can be reached by email: bridges@pchg.net; phone/fax: (1-902) 897 6665; mailing address: 14 Court St, Suite 101, Truro, Nova Scotia, B2N 3H7, Canada.

2. One of the creators of the Power and Control Wheel, Ellen Pence (1999) also seems to be moving away from thinking of the power and control story as a grand narrative that can explain battering in its entirety. Pence (1999) writes, 'It was the cases themselves that created the chink in each of our theoretical suits of armour. Speaking for myself, I found that many of the men I interviewed did not seem to articulate a desire for power over their female partner. Although I relentlessly took every opportunity to point out to the men in the groups that they were so motivated and merely in denial ...' (p.29).

3. I want to acknowledge Art Fisher of Alternatives – A Domestic Abuse Intervention Program, Bridgewater, Nova Scotia, Canada for our collaboration in identifying dichotomous thinking in our work.

4. The research involves interviews I conducted with six of my colleagues, in Nova Scotia, Canada, who work with men who batter. I interviewed the counsellors at their place of work which meant travelling to locations throughout Nova Scotia. All the counsellors work for intervention programs funded by the Nova Scotia Department of Community Services. I conducted semi-structured ninety minute interviews with two female and four male counsellors based on a prepared outline. To ensure the anonymity of those involved, all names have been changed and identifying information omitted.

5. In contrast, Goldner (1998) finds it helpful to notice how the abuse is often both calculated and uncalculated, how the men are often both 'in control' and 'out of control'. She writes: 'from a both/and perspective, violence is best conceptualized as simultaneously wilful and impulse-ridden, as both instrumental and dissociative ... treatment is most effective in helping men take responsibility for being violent when the therapist can rhetorically encompass both the intentional and impulsive

dimensions of their experience' (p.279). She works with the man in a way that both expands the man's self-description (i.e., noticing his agency and responsibility) without negating his experience. To acknowledge both positions she asks the men questions like, 'What made you choose to lose it?', 'Can you remember the moment when you chose to lose it?'(p.279).

6. I appreciate researcher John P. McKendy's (1997) observation that the men's experiences of social injustice such as class are often 'seen-but-unnoticed' (p.135) in some work with men who abuse in intimate relationships.

7. Mahoney (1994) writes, 'in our society, agency and victimization are each known by the absence of the other: you are an agent if you are not a victim, and you are not a victim if you are in anyway an agent ... This all-agent or all-victim conceptual dichotomy will not be easy to escape or transform' (p.64).

8. This perpetrator/victim dichotomy also reinforced the idea that the violence was 'working' (vs. 'not working') and the idea that the men know 'exactly what they are doing'. To suggest that the violence was somehow 'not working' or that the men did not know 'exactly what they were doing' was to risk defining them as victims. We thought that defining the men as 'victims' of their own violence might in some way absolve them of their responsibility for it. Therefore, in an effort to hold the men responsible within this dichotomous framework, we thought we had to emphasise the violence 'working' and the men 'knowing exactly what they were doing' and de-emphasised the negative effects of the violence on the men.

9. Some feminist writers (Kitzinger & Perkins 1993) have pointed out the ways in which the word 'safety' has been co-opted by psychological language. '"Safety" is one of the many words that has been taken over by psychology and its meaning fundamentally altered. The concept of "safety" has a history in the battered women's movement, in which safety meant escape from her batterer, a shelter' (p.145). They point out that while safety once meant a real place where a woman can go to get away from a man's fist, or knife, or gun, now it is seen as anything required to make an individual *feel* safe.

10. I appreciate Michael White's ideas on this issue: 'It's really not enough for these men to just take responsibility for the abuse ... It is *important to establish a context* in which it becomes possible for these men to separate from some of the dominant ways of being and thinking that inform the abuse ... But even this is not enough. It is crucial that we engage with these men in the exploration of *alternative ways of being* and thinking that bring with them new proposals for action in their relationships with their women partners and with their children, and that these proposals be accountable to these women and children [emphasis added].' (McLean 1994, p.71)

References

Adams, D. 1988: 'A profeminist analysis of treatment models of men who batter.' In K. Yllo & M. Bograd (eds): *Feminist perspectives on wife abuse*, pp.176-199. Beverly Hills: Sage.

Augusta-Scott, T. 1999: 'Reinventing the wheel: Finding new stories for men who batter.' Master's Thesis. Dalhousie University, Halifax, Nova Scotia.

Emerge 2000: *Emerge Batterers Intervention Group Program Manual.* Cambridge, Massachusetts: Emerge, Inc.

Fineman, M. & Mykitick, R. (eds) 1994: *The Public Nature of Private Violence: The discovery of domestic abuse.* New York: Routledge.

Goldner, V., Penn, P., Sheinberg, M. & Walker, G. 1990: 'Love and violence: Gender paradoxes in volatile attachments.' *Family Process*, 29(4):343-364.

Goldner. V. 1998: 'The treatment of violence and victimization in intimate relationships.' *Family Process*, 37(3):263-286.

Jenkins, A. 1998. 'Invitations to responsibility: Engaging adolescents and young men who have sexually abused.' In Marshall et al. (eds): *Handbook for treatment of sexual offenders*, pp.163-189. San Francisco: Jossey-Bass.

Jenkins, A. 1997: 'Alcohol and men's violence: An interview with Alan Jenkins.' *Dulwich Centre Newsletter*, Nos.2&3, pp.43-47.

Jenkins, A. 1996. 'Moving towards respect: A quest for balance.' In C. McLean, M. Carey & C. While (eds): *Men's Ways of Being*, pp.117–133. Boulder, Colorado: Westview Press.

Jenkins, A. 1994. 'Therapy for abuse or therapy as abuse.' *Dulwich Centre Newsletter*, No.1, pp.11-19.

Jenkins, A. 1991: 'Intervention with violence and abuse in families: The inadvertent perpetuation of irresponsible behavior.' *Australia and New Zealand Journal of Family Therapy*, 2(4):186-195.

Jenkins, A. 1990: *Invitations to Responsibility: The therapeutic engagement of men who are violent and abuse.* Adelaide, South Australia: Dulwich Centre Publications.

Jones, A. 1994: 'Where do we go from here?' *Ms*, Sept./Oct. pp.56-63.

Kane, T., Staiger, P. & Ricciardelli, L. 2000: 'Male domestic violence: Attitudes, aggression, and interpersonal dependency.' *Journal of Interpersonal Violence*, 15(1):16-29.

Kaufman, M. 1987: 'The construction of masculinity and the triad of men's violence.' In Kaufman, M. (ed): *Beyond Patriarchy: Essays by men on pleasure, power, and change.* Toronto: Oxford University Press.

Kaufman, M. (ed) 1987: *Beyond Patriarchy: Essays by men on pleasure, power, and change.* Toronto: Oxford University Press.

Kitzinger C. & Perkins, R. 1993: *Changing Our Minds: Lesbian feminism and psychology.* New York University Press. London.

Mahoney, M. 1994: 'Victimization or oppression? Women's lives, violence, and agency.' In Fineman, M. & Mykitiuk, R. (eds): *The Public Nature of Private Violence: The discovery of domestic abuse.* New York: Routledge

McKendy, J.P. 1997: 'The class politics of domestic violence.' *Journal of Sociology and Social Welfare*, XXIV(3):135-155.

McLean, C. 1994: 'A conversation about accountability with Michael White.' *Dulwich Centre Newsletter*, Nos.2&3, pp.68-79.

Mederos, F. 1999: 'Batterer intervention programs: The past and future prospects.' In E. Pence & M. Shepard (eds): *Coordinating community responses to domestic violence: Lessons from duluth and beyond*, pp.127–150. Newbury Park, CA: Sage.

Paymar, M. 2000: *Violent No More: Helping men end domestic abuse.* Revised Second Edition. Alameda, California: Hunter House Inc.

Pence, E. 1999: 'Some thoughts on philosophy.' In E. Pence & M. Shepard (eds), *Coordinating Community Responses to Domestic Violence: Lessons from Duluth and beyond*, pp.25–40. Thousand Oaks, CA: Sage.

Pence, E. & Shepard, M. 1999: *Coordinating Community Responses to Domestic Violence: Lessons from Duluth and beyond.* Thousand Oaks, CA: Sage.

Pence, E. & Paymar, M. 1993: *Education Groups for Men Who Batter: The Duluth model.* New York: Springer.

Schechter, S. 1982: *Women and Male Violence: The visions and struggles of the battered women's movement.* Boston, MA: South End Press.

13.

Alcohol
and
men's violence

an interview with

Alan Jenkins[1]

I think that there is a great deal of mythology about the relationship between alcohol and violence in our culture. Alcohol is frequently seen by the community, and in professional and scientific literature, as a causal factor in producing violence. These attributions have been made as a result of the association of' alcohol abuse' with other forms of abuse, including violence and sexual assault. Research literature indicates that up to 70% of incidents of violence are associated with use of alcohol. There is often a leap from the acknowledgment of this association to attributions of causality. The people involved are believed to be violent *because* of their alcohol use. There is no doubt that alcohol leads to sloppy behaviour and sloppy thinking. However, it requires an extraordinary leap in credibility to suggest that alcohol use somehow causes violence. In my work with men who enact violence and abusive behaviour, I find it extremely unhelpful to attribute a causal link between alcohol use and violence.

Men who enact violence tend to engage with a range of ideas, preoccupations and thinking practices that are self-righteous, blaming, vengeful and contemptuous about other individuals or subcultures. Some invest in sexually exploitative preoccupations which are increasingly self-centred and insensitive to the actual feelings and experience of others. It is these thinking patterns that create a context for violence and abuse. In my work with men who enact violence or abuse I have found that they tend to 'work themselves up' with these self-righteous, blaming and vengeful preoccupations. They 'intoxicate themselves' with a range of ideas, a range of attributions of blame, and give themselves a range of permissions to hurt other people.

Violence and abusive behaviour are the result of active choices which are informed by sequences of self-centred preoccupation, rationalisation and justification. These ideas and preoccupations are in turn informed by dominant cultural ideologies which relate to beliefs about entitlement, privilege and power and expectations of deference and submission from those regarded as inferior or of lesser status. Within this context, I have tried to understand the association between violence and alcohol use. Many individuals who have been drinking heavily give themselves, and are given by others, a special kind of permission to act in irresponsible ways. A range of minimisations, justifications and excuses for irresponsible behaviour become available.

The constructions of responsibility, when alcohol or drugs are involved, are quite different than in other circumstances. This is illustrated by expressions like: 'He's an angry drunk', 'When I'm drunk I lose it', 'I was drunk, I didn't know what I was doing'. We construct specific meanings and attributions of responsibility in the context of alcohol use. Men who drink and abuse engage in a kind of tautological thinking whereby they often give themselves permission to engage in violence when they drink. Later their behaviour may be excused and tolerated by others because they were drunk.

Constructions of responsibility

Constructions of responsibility inform and often determine expressions of behaviour. If individuals believe, 'When I'm drunk I lose it', or 'I would never do that if I was sober', then that is exactly how they behave. The thinking is tautological and the idea becomes the reality.

Many men are quite clear about[1] their responsibilities regarding violence and respectful behaviour in relationships. They may drink alcohol and make respectful and responsible decisions about how, when, and where they drink and how they behave in those circumstances. Even within the lives of men who enact violence and alcohol abuse, there are generally many examples of times when they have been drinking and have engaged in responsible and respectful behaviour. They may be described as being violent only when they are drunk. However, when their day-to-day experiences are explored, it is generally evident that they engage in patterns of vengeful and self-righteous thinking, and enact behaviours influenced by these ways of thinking, at times when they have not been drinking.

Instead of explaining the association between alcohol use and violence in terms of a causal link, I am much more interested in exploring attributions of responsibility in the circumstances of violence and in the circumstances of alcohol abuse.

Inviting responsibility

When working with men who engage in violence and alcohol or substance abuse, I try to separate the two issues and invite a focus on individual responsibility. This does not require confrontation by directly challenging causal attributions. Whether or not he believes his violence is due to his alcohol use, I am interested in the influence that violence and alcohol abuse may each be having on his relationships and his own self-respect. The influence of both can be helpfully and independently explored in the light of the man's preferences and desires. I am particularly interested in discovering and clarifying the kind of relationships that he is wanting, and highlighting the influence of violence and alcohol abuse upon qualities such as respect, trust, safely, desire, integrity, etc. I tend to decline invitations to challenge causal connections between violence and alcohol but invite exploration of their influences upon the man's goals and relationship preferences.

Many men express preferences and desires for respectful relationships which are based on mutuality rather than fear or duty and qualities which include safety, trust and non-violence. Violence and alcohol abuse can both be seen to involve behaviours which are distancing the man from his own stated preferences. I invite him to undertake a journey to face his violence; to examine and detail his violence. I invite him to discover the patterns of thinking that he reproduces at different stages of the times of his violence; how he 'works himself up' with patterns of self-righteous thinking and attribution of blame towards his partner and her behaviour. When starting to explore these patterns of thinking and behaviour, it becomes increasingly clear that these are not patterns of experience that are unique to times when he is drinking. In fact some men acknowledge ways in which drinking can become a specific way of avoiding responsibility. Some men drink following feelings of self-disgust after having engaged in violence or abusive behaviour.

By starting to invite the man to study his own patterns of thinking and behaviour, an opportunity is created for him to begin to realise that self-righteous, blaming and controlling ideas and preoccupations can influence patterns of both violence and substance use and that they have a life and expression beyond the times when he is drinking. Both violence and alcohol use become parallel issues rather than being seen as causally related. Men who cling to causal attributions can be invited to consider and clarify their responsibilities with respect to both. If an association is postulated, what responsibility is the man taking to ensure that he is never affected by alcohol in the presence of his family?

Men who engage in either domestic abuse or 'alcohol abuse' have generally been quite reliant on other people in their lives to monitor their behaviour for them; it may be a partner, a mother or another family member. These family members can generally articulate very clearly how the man 'works himself up'. They know when to 'walk on eggshells' around him, they study his behaviour and know when it is and is not safe to speak out. They have learned to study his behaviour for their own safety and survival. The man has tended to rely on their efforts and has generally paid little attention to the processes of 'self-intoxication' in which he engages. Consequently he is extremely ignorant about his own experience and the ways in which he 'works himself up'. He feels that he suddenly 'loses it' or 'snaps'. However, as he begins to study this process himself, rather than leave it to others, he enables himself to begin to take responsibility for his own actions.

Violence as addiction

A number of popular models to address violence and abusive behaviour rely on a model of explanation that uses the metaphor of 'addiction'. Various forms of violence are described in language of 'compulsivity' and addiction. These explanations do not serve only to *describe* an individual's experience of having a problem with violence over which he feels he has no control. By constructing the problem in these terms, such explanations also serve to *create* the experience of 'addiction'. There are many ways of understanding violence in our culture that promote this experience of 'lack of control'. Many men who enact violence believe that they have a quality such as 'aggression', 'an overactive sex drive' or a 'short fuse' in their character or personality. This quality is seen to 'take them over' or 'let them down'. Such men experience themselves as being overwhelmed by a force outside of their control. Psychologists describe personality disorders which are based on notions of character excesses or deficits such as 'impulsiveness' or 'compulsiveness'. The identities of these men are confused with their actions; they are labelled as 'perpetrators', perhaps with 'limited impulse control'.

What happens to responsibility in this context? These constructions lead people to attribute responsibility for violence and abusive behaviour to factors outside of their control. It is hardly surprising that individuals come to see themselves as helpless in the face of strong urges and overwhelmed by their own experience. It is only a short step to adopting the metaphor of' addiction'. The concept of addiction can be a comforting one because it excuses the man of responsibility for his actions and avoids the necessity for self-examination and facing the inevitable feelings of shame which accompany the acceptance of culpability and choice.

These constructions constrain any discovery and acknowledgment of the practices of 'self-intoxication' and the preoccupations and investments into particular ways of thinking. They also obscure the ideologies or cultural restraints which inform practices of' self-intoxication' and violence. For example, cultural notions about male sexuality which include notions of sexual inevitability, performance and conquest promote the idea that men are slaves to their own arousal and not responsible for its consequences. These ideas inform practices of sexual violence. Metaphors of addiction not only obscure notions of individual responsibility and individual choice but can also blind us to broader cultural responsibilities and priorities. There are any number of twelve-step programs for 'sex and love addicts', and so on, which can serve to reinforce these ideas.

Concepts of addiction can be quite dangerous when applied to issues of men's violence and abusive behaviour. They fail to promote a sense of agency for the man to set limits and take responsibility for his own behaviour. They don't encourage him to examine his own thinking and behaviour and to notice and attend to patterns of thinking and ways in which he 'works himself up' to justify the use of violence and abusive behaviour. They don't encourage him to examine anything about the cultural context hi which he lives and the ways in which he constructs experience.

Control: losing it or enacting it?

The notion of 'losing control' or 'losing it' is extremely prevalent. Many men who engage in violence or abusive behaviour understand their experience in terms of having 'lost control'. They experience something 'coming over them', 'sweeping over them', 'taking them over', or something 'coming up inside of them' and 'overwhelming them'. They adopt an extremely passive stance. Many models of individual psychology collude with these sorts of ideas. They describe people as being like containers or pressure systems hi which forces build up inside of them. There is an inherent passivity in these metaphors. They prescribe solutions which require men to 'let it out' or 'let off steam' by going for a run or punching a punching bag, etc. They obscure the active process whereby the man makes choices and gradually 'intoxicates himself with his own self-righteous thinking.

The process of 'working oneself up' is an active process in which individuals invest. I am interested in inviting men to gradually examine their own participation in developing patterns of self-righteousness or sexually exploitative thinking. Examination of these processes in turn highlights cultural ideas that inform the thinking. These ideas can then be located in a context of ideology about power and privilege in the broader culture. Certain people feel entitled to become self-righteous and enrage themselves about others who are accorded less status as a result of factors including age, gender, social class, race, etc. Some men take permission to arouse themselves at the expense of individuals who are sexually objectified and systematically taken advantage of. An awareness of processes which enable the translation of unjust cultural ideology into self-righteous and exploitative preoccupations enables the deconstruction of practices of violence and abuse and the discovery of concepts of choice, responsibility and personal agency.

The man can examine his thinking and behaviour in ways that he has never done before but in reference to his own goals and preferences. He can begin to develop an understanding of an active process on his part, his own contribution, his own participation in both the problem and the solution. He can choose to experiment with ways of varying and changing that participation by challenging habits and processes of 'self-intoxication'. If he has relied on other people to do that thinking for him in the past, he can start to do it for himself. He can examine and evaluate the cultural ideas that have informed his actions. A sense of agency is promoted by these activities. He will also begin to notice times when he has made respectful choices, when he has resisted self-righteous thinking and acted respectfully, sometimes in challenging circumstances. He will begin to discover his capacity for respectful choices and behaviour.

Ironically, instead of feeling that he 'loses control', he may begin to realise that he has in fact been enacting forms of controlling behaviour towards others. His abusive actions might be re- interpreted as desperate efforts to establish or maintain control of others. Men who examine patterns of sexually abusive preoccupation and behaviour in detail soon come to 'see it like it really is' rather than regarding themselves as victims of circumstances beyond their control. Sexually abusive behaviour is frequently constituted by a series of tactical decisions and choices which are designed to set up, trick and entrap the 'participation' of the person who is victimised. Men who abuse can be invited to deconstruct their behaviour and examine their thinking and actions in terms of strategies and active choices. These constructions, which can enable a sense of responsibility, are frequently obscured in models of addiction.

I find it helpful to invite men who have abused to discover and examine their own influence in their lives rather than see themselves as under the influence of a condition, disorder or substance over which they have no control. This enables the construction of responsibility in a manner which is accessible and achievable. The metaphor of addiction requires the man to acknowledge that he is powerless in the face of his problem and can thereby place responsibility outside of his control.

Choice, responsibility, and hope

Notions of addiction invite constructions of deviance which relate to individual pathology, limited choice and external attributions of responsibility. We need metaphors and models for explanation and intervention which enable choice and personal responsibility and which invite examination of the cultural ideologies which inform practices of violence and abusive behaviour. We are all influenced by dominant ideologies of individualism, competition, blame and avoidance of responsibility for our own actions. We need explanatory models which expose these notions and the thinking practices associated with them, not mystify them or disguise them as individual pathology. We don't need any more ways to categorise people into hierarchies of competence and ability and then deny them the opportunities to develop their own preferred ways of relating. Effective intervention needs to take violence out of a context of pathology and into a broader context that examines the ways in which ideology informs behaviour, and invites personal choice and personal responsibility.

The metaphor of addiction promotes a sense of helplessness and reliance upon others to take responsibility. If I adopted this construction, I would also be colluding with a range of cultural ideas which suggest that men who abuse can't help themselves. This would engender a sense of helplessness and justification for practices of violence. The only solution appears to be to submit to a superior force and seek external direction. This dilemma is not new to many of the men with whom I work who are struggling in their relationships with external 'authorities'. They don't need to submit to being taken over by another external influence but instead need to discover their own influence in their lives. When men who consult with me believe that 'they lose it', they don't see any direction that they can take other than encouraging other people to change around them. I often feel invited to perceive the world in the same way and to join in that sense of hopelessness. It feels like an impossible situation with no direction. However, to work together to construct a context for responsibility enables a sense of agency where the man can make choices, where he can examine the tactical nature of violence and abusive behaviour, where he faces the shame that accompanies empathy with the experience of those he has hurt; these directions all seem to offer the possibility to discover more respectful ways of living. They offer the possibility to make restitution to others and to himself. They offer hope of realising the man's own preferences and goals.

Notes

This paper, which was created from an interview with Dulwich Centre Publications' staff writer David Denborough, was first published in the *Dulwich Centre Newsletter*, 1997 Nos.2&3. Republished here with permission.

1. Alan Jenkins can be contacted c/o Nada, 1 Mary Street, Hindmarsh SA 5009, Australia. Alan has written a number of published papers, including the book entitled: *Invitations to Responsibility: The therapeutic engagement of men who are violent and abusive* (Dulwich Centre Publications 1990).